The Rise and Fall of the Ottoman Empire: The History of the Turkish Empire's Creation and Its Destruction Over 600 Years Later

By Charles River Editors

A picture of the Ottoman flag

About Charles River Editors

Charles River Editors is a boutique digital publishing company, specializing in bringing history back to life with educational and engaging books on a wide range of topics. Keep up to date with our new and free offerings with this 5 second sign up on our weekly mailing list, and visit Our Kindle Author Page to see other recently published Kindle titles.

We make these books for you and always want to know our readers' opinions, so we encourage you to leave reviews and look forward to publishing new and exciting titles each week.

Introduction

15th century depiction of the Ottoman siege of Constantinople

The Rise of the Ottoman Empire

In terms of geopolitics, perhaps the most seminal event of the Middle Ages was the successful Ottoman siege of Constantinople in 1453. The city had been an imperial capital as far back as the 4th century, when Constantine the Great shifted the power center of the Roman Empire there, effectively establishing two almost equally powerful halves of antiquity's greatest empire. Constantinople would continue to serve as the capital of the Byzantine Empire even after the Western half of the Roman Empire collapsed in the late 5th century. Naturally, the Ottoman Empire would also use Constantinople as the capital of its empire after their conquest effectively ended the Byzantine Empire, and thanks to its strategic location, it has been a trading center for years and remains one today under the Turkish name of Istanbul.

The end of the Byzantine Empire had a profound effect not only on the Middle East but Europe as well. Constantinople had played a crucial part in the Crusades, and the fall of the Byzantines meant that the Ottomans now shared a border with Europe. The Islamic empire was viewed as a threat by the predominantly Christian continent to their west, and it took little time for different European nations to start clashing with the powerful Turks. In fact, the Ottomans would clash with Russians, Austrians, Venetians, Polish, and more before collapsing as a result of World War I, when they were part of the Central powers.

The Ottoman conquest of Constantinople also played a decisive role in fostering the Renaissance in Western Europe. The Byzantine Empire's influence had helped ensure that it was the custodian of various ancient texts, most notably from the ancient Greeks, and when Constantinople fell, Byzantine refugees flocked west to seek refuge in Europe. Those refugees brought books that helped spark an interest in antiquity that fueled the Italian Renaissance and essentially put an end to the Middle Ages altogether.

The long agony of the "sick man of Europe,"[1] an expression used by the Tsar of Russia to depict the falling Ottomans, could almost blind people to its incredible power and history. Preserving its mixed heritage, coming from both its geographic position rising above the ashes of the Byzantine Empire and the tradition inherited from the Muslim Conquests, the Ottoman Empire lasted more than six centuries. Its soldiers fought, died, and conquered lands on three different continents, making it one of the few stable multi-ethnic empires in history - and likely one of the last. Thus, it's somewhat inevitable that the history of its dissolution is at the heart of complex geopolitical disputes, as well as sectarian tensions that are still key to understanding the Middle East, North Africa and the Balkans.

When studying the fall of the Ottoman Empire, historians have argued over the breaking point that saw a leading global power slowly become a decadent empire. The failed Battle of Vienna in 1683 is certainly an important turning point for the expanding empire; the defeat of Grand Vizier Kara Mustafa Pasha at the hands of a coalition led by the Austrian Habsburg dynasty, Holy Roman Empire and Polish-Lithuanian commonwealth marked the end of Ottoman expansionism. It was also the beginning of a slow decline during which the Ottoman Empire suffered multiple military defeats, found itself mired by corruption, and had to deal with the increasingly mutinous Janissaries (the Empire's initial foot soldiers).

Despite it all, the Ottoman Empire would survive for over 200 more years, and in the last century of its life it strove to reform its military, administration and economy until it was finally dissolved. Years before the final collapse of the Empire, the Tanzimat ("Reorganization"), a period of swiping reforms, led to significant changes in the country's military apparatus, among others, which certainly explains the initial success the Ottoman Empire was able to achieve against its rivals. Similarly, the drafting of a new Constitution (*Kanûn-u Esâsî*, basic law) in 1876, despite it being shot down by Sultan Abdul Hamid II just two years later, as well as its revival by the "Young Turks" movement in 1908, highlights the understanding among Ottoman elites that change was needed, and their belief that such change was possible.

Looking at the events of the empire's last two centuries, and interpreting the fall of the Ottoman Empire as a slow but long decline is what could be called the "accepted narrative." At the start of World War I, the Ottoman Empire was often described as a dwindling power, mired by administrative corruption, using inferior technology, and plagued by poor leadership. The general idea is that the Ottoman Empire was "lagging behind," likely coming from the clear stagnation of the Empire between 1683 and 1826. Yet it can be argued that this portrayal is often misleading and fails to give a fuller picture of the state of the Ottoman Empire. The fact that the other existing multicultural Empire, namely the Austro-Hungarian Empire, also did not survive World War I should put into question this "accepted narrative." Looking at the reforms, technological advances and modernization efforts made by the Ottoman elite between 1826 and the beginning of World War I, one could really wonder why such a thirst for change failed to save the Ottomans when similar measures taken by other nations, such as Japan during the Meiji era, did in fact result in the rise of a global power in the 20th century.

During the period that preceded its collapse, the Ottoman Empire was at the heart of a growing rivalry between two of the competing global powers of the time, England and France. The two powers asserted their influence over a declining empire, the history of which is anchored in Europe as much as in Asia. However, while the two powers were instrumental in the final defeat and collapse of the Ottoman Empire, their stance toward what came to be known as the "Eastern Question" – the fate of the Ottoman Empire – is not one of clear enmity. Both England and France found, at times, reasons to extend the life of the sick man of Europe until it finally sided with their shared enemies. Russia's stance toward the Ottoman Empire is much more clear-cut; the rising Asian and European powers saw the Ottomans as a rival, which they strove to contain, divide and finally destroy for more than 300 years in a series of wars against their old adversary.

Last but not least, the rise of nationalism among peoples under Ottoman domination was a key factor in the dissolution of the empire. At the end of the 19th century, shortly before its final collapse, the territory of the Ottoman Empire dwindled due to the growing call for independence coming from different ethnicities it ruled for hundreds of years. The Empire's inclusiveness, which marked it as a direct successor of the Byzantine Empire, was most certainly challenged by an aging leadership. The Ottoman Empire's inability to create a shared identity, a weak central state, and growing inner dissensions were some of the main factors explaining its long demise. Such a failure also explains the need for the creation of a new form of identity, which was ultimately provided by Mustafa Kemal, the founding father of modern Turkey.

Overall, the history of the dissolution can be defined as a race between the Empire's growing "illness" on one side (the Ottoman's inability to appease and federate the various people within its territory), and constant attempts to find a cure in the form of broad reforms. These questions are often presented together, but that tends to shift the focus outward, onto the various peoples and their aspirations, along with Europe's growing influence over the fate of the Ottoman Empire. To consider both the "illness" and the cure, it's necessary to separate them, before moving on to the direct cause of the empire's dissolution (World War I) and its heritage.

The Rise and Fall of the Ottoman Empire: The History of the Turkish Empire's Creation and Its Destruction Over 600 Years Later chronicles the rise and fall of one of history's most influential empires. Along with pictures of important people, places, and events, you will learn about the rise and fall of the Ottoman Empire like never before.

Anatolia and the Byzantine Empire

Previous to the existence of the Ottoman Empire, there were two dominating powers in the area, both of which the Ottomans had to conquer in order to grow into the empire it would become.

The Byzantine Empire existed for over a thousand years with a history spanning from the division of the Roman Empire in 395 until the conquest of Constantinople in 1453. It was formed from the previous Eastern Roman Empire and during its long existence, the Byzantine inhabitants were very proud to call themselves Romans. However, many things changed during the long lifespan of the Byzantine Empire, starting with a Hellenization in the 6th century. The use of the Latin language diminished and Greek took its place, while the typical Roman culture gave way to a more Hellenistic. The Hellenization of Byzantium was detrimental to the relationship with the Holy Roman Empire and the Christian world from that point would be split in two. The strengthening of the Orthodox Church caused many civil wars and conflicts to arise during the centuries which shattered and reshaped the territory time after time. By the end of the Byzantine Empire's existence, the old age had weakened both the state and church, making it an easy target for invading forces.

Such an invading group was, among others, the Turkish-speaking Seljuks, lead through a series of battles by Kutalmishouglu Suleiman who supported different usurpers against the Byzantine emperor. The expansion of the Seljuks was successful and when Suleiman died he had put all of Bithynia under his control as well as several important harbor towns along the shores on the Asian side of Bosphorus. With that accomplishment, he had managed to separate the Byzantines living in Anatolia from their emperor in Constantinople. This immediately weakened the unity of the Byzantine Empire.

When another invading Muslim army took control of what today is Syria, Israel, and Northern Africa, the dismembered Byzantine Empire lost significant portions of land but instead grew into a smaller and stronger unity. It took a lot of power struggles and battles on many fronts for the empire to recapture some of the lands, though control over Anatolia was shared with the Seljuk Sultanate of Rum. Gradually the Byzantine Empire lost all influence in Anatolia and by the end of the 11th century, the Hellenic culture and Greek language were replaced by Islam and Turkish.

The Sultanate of Rum was an independent state in the Seljuk Empire and united many different tribes under one rule. While the Seljuk Empire was heavily influenced by Persian culture and language the Sultanate of Rum kept its Turkish traditions and roots and also postponed adopting the new religion spreading in the area, Islam. Though the Seljuk Empire didn't last for as many years as the neighboring Byzantine it was crucial for the unification of the area, thus paving way for the future overtake by the Ottomans and making the transition of power slightly smoother.

Both the empires were still in existence when the Ottoman seed was planted in what today is western Turkey. As the Seljuk Sultanate of Rum grew in power and absorbed more and more of the neighboring states, with ports on both the Black Sea and the Mediterranean, the Byzantine Empire was frequently invaded both from the north and south. It stood on its height by the end of the 10th century with large land masses in what today is Bulgaria, the Balkans, south of Italy, parts of Romania and most of Turkey. People in the subjugated states were dissatisfied with the ruthlessness of the Orthodox Church and the violence by which it had conquered them. The acrimony of the defeated Bulgars and Armenians made their loyalty vane, and they didn't put up much resistance when the Ottoman finally arrived.

The Seljuks controlled some of the trade passing by on the road stretching all the way from the ports of Genua in the Holy Roman Empire, via the Mediterranean Sea, into Anatolia and further on along the Silk Road through Central Asia to China. Not just wares but also science, medicine, philosophy, and culture were exchanged along the route making the area prosperous and progressive. The multicultural exchange had positive impacts on minority groups in the region. During the Seljuk takeover and later on the Ottoman Empire, Christians and Jews were most of the time not proselytized to the Islamic faith. In fact, a big part of the European Jewish population fled from the violent spread of Christianity to the Muslim territories in Anatolia. Both Christians and Jews were allowed to practice their religion within the Muslim community, although as secondary citizens. In contrast, the Christian Holy Roman Empire fought ruthlessly against indigenous beliefs, Muslims, and Jewish people. In the east, The Sultanate of Rum kept its firm grip of Anatolia and withstood three attacking crusades sent by the Holy Roman Empire between 1096 and 1192. It wasn't until the Mongols first struck the sultanate at Erzurum in 1242 that the Sultanate started to decline and soon fell apart. The Turks had to swear allegiance to the Mongols while the sultan fled to the Byzantine Balkans. After his death a few years later the Sultanate of Rum was divided into smaller emirates, so-called beyliks, of which the Ottoman family ruled one.

The clash between the Orthodox Byzantine Empire and the Catholic Holy Roman Empire persisted and instead of assisting their Christian brothers in fighting back the bellicose invaders, the Catholic Church contributed to Byzantine's grievances. Pope Urban II urged his devotees to head to the Holy Land of Jerusalem and take it back from the heathen Muslims.

A depiction of Pope Urban II calling for a crusade

This led to the First Crusade in 1096, which had a damaging effect on the Byzantine Empire. One result of the long crusades was the foundation of several minor crusader states, populated by Franks and Romans within the territory. These states interfered with and disrupted the Byzantine Empire while also occupying their lands. The empire had to put up with several more crusades passing by, and even though the crusader's incentive was to conquer Jerusalem and rid the lands of the Seljuks, the ruthless behavior of the troops merely led to annoyance and disputes between the Orthodox Christians and the Catholics. The third crusade was the culmination of these disputes and the Byzantine emperor made a secret alliance with his former enemies. The Seljuks, now led by the infamous Saladin promised to help him fight back the crusader Frederick Barbarossa. After this scheme became known to the Holy Roman Empire, the next crusade led to the Sack of Constantinople 1204, making the capital a crusader state under Catholic rule. Though

Constantinople later was returned to the Byzantine Empire, all the commotion the crusades had created during these 200 years was irreversible. The empire was already weakened and in the 14th century, two fatal civil wars diminished its military power and gradually made it an easy target for surrounding enemies. The start of the decline somewhat coincided with the Mongol conquest of the Seljuks in the 13th century, and the whole area was shattered and divided by the mid 14th century. As Byzantine, the Seljuk Empire and the Sultanate of Rum all had succumbed to external and internal wars during these tumultuous centuries, the territory was largely up for grabs by anyone willing to restore the region's former glory and build a new empire.

The timing was ideal for the Ottoman Empire to fill the power void left by the former empires.

The Ottomans

The origins of the Ottoman Empire and the dynasty that founded it are surrounded by legends and mysteries. The mythology around Osman I and his closest family created an image of the dynasty, legitimizing their heritage and right to rule. While some of it surely is true, a lot of it may also be sheer exaggeration. Even the true origin of the Ottoman dynasty is heavily debated by modern historians. The general opinion is that the Ottomans descended from the Kayi tribe, a branch of the Oghuz Turks. This was never mentioned in any records actually written by the time of Osman I's life, but firstly 200 years later, which makes it a highly contested statement. Contemporaneous writers would claim Osman to be a descendant of the Kayi tribe to aggrandize him.

The Kayi Tribe was powerful, prosperous and played an important role in the Caucasus region, both at the time before Osman was born and for hundreds of years to come. To link the Ottoman dynasty with such a tribe would work as an incentive to keep up good relations with the actual Kayi tribe, and also inflate the story about how the Ottoman dynasty descended from power and political influence. It would also support the inherited right of the Ottoman dynasty to rule the area. Though this may never be clearly settled amongst historians today, we do know that Osman's family was one of many Oghuz Turkish people originating from what today is western Kazakhstan, just east of the Caspian Sea.

From there, the Seljuk tribe of Oghuz people moved southwest into Persia and founded their empire, slowly moving west towards the Byzantine Empire. When the Seljuk Empire disintegrated, many smaller states were formed all over Anatolia and Osman's father Ertugrul was a ruler of one of them. Legend has it that Ertugrul and his army of 400 horse-borne fighters accidentally came upon a battle between two foreign armies. Heroically he decided to intervene and support the side currently losing. With his help, they turned the battle and won. Ertugrul learned that he had been fighting on the side of the Sultan of Konya, from the capital of Rum, against the invading forces of the Mongolian armies.

As a reward for his actions, he was handed a piece of land in northwestern Anatolia, centered around the town of Sögut. The truth in this story is again under debate since it wasn't written down until much later. There is no clear evidence of how Ertugrul came in possession of the lands he ruled or what his relationship was with the Sultanate of Rum. All we can say for sure is that this became the embryo of the Ottoman Empire as Ertugrul settled down, got married and later also had a son, Osman. This happened sometime in the middle of the 13th century, but the exact date of Osman's birth was never recorded.

During the years of Osman's childhood, his father was the chief of his given lands but also subordinated the Sultanate of Rum. When Osman was 23, his father died and Osman inherited the title and power Ertugrul had earned. It was now nearing the end of the 13th century and the Sultanate of Rum, as well as the whole Seljuk Empire, was disintegrating. The rise and expansion of Osman's territory came more or less as a natural consequence, replacing one power with another. It was a gradual process going on for generations of the Ottoman dynasty and Osman's early conquerings were only a fraction of how large the empire would become. The necessity of expansion was in later years explained with the spreading of the Muslim faith. The truth behind this is a contaminated topic among modern historians and hard to verify. Islam is no longer considered to be a driving force for either Ertugrul or Osman. Ertugrul was not a Muslim, but many claim Osman's religious father-in-law converted him to the faith. The story of how Osman became a devout Muslim is of importance to the Ottoman legacy. It includes a prophecy where God himself appoints Osman and his descendants to glory and success. This was in later centuries used to legitimize the continued rule of his heirs. It was also Osman who named the whole empire and the following dynasty, still alive today. Osman is the Arabic version of the Turkish Uthman, or Athman, which scholars believe was Osman's real name. His name changed into Osman under influence from the Arabic and Persian Islamic culture, to signal his transcendence into a Muslim. Whether or not Osman was religious he decided to expand into Byzantine territory and kept peace with his Turkish neighbors. Until the actual dissolution of the Seljuk Empire, the Ottoman dynasty did not fight other Turkish tribes.

The Rise and Reign of Osman I

To try to pinpoint the descent and origins of the Ottoman dynasty and Osman himself is more or less impossible today. The sources are highly contaminated with propaganda like factoids about Osman's persona, his heroic actions and the constant success of his ambitions, written at the height of the Ottoman Empire hundreds of years after Osman's reign. There are hardly any actual records from his childhood and we know very little about his early years of conquest. Probably because at the time being, Osman's father and family were not considered particularly mighty or influential. Thus, the lack of contemporaneous writings implies the falsehood of the anachronistic records speaking of Osman's visions and also of his father's heroic intervention against the Mongol army. Anatolia consisted of many beyliks at the time, as well as different alliances between tribes from all over Eurasia, Eastern Europe, Middle East and as far away as

Central Asia. The number of interconnections and movements between the different tribes are uncountable, which makes it harder to factually pin down the true origins of Osman's ancestors. Whoever the ascendants of Osman truly were one can safely say that his descendants, using his very name, would be well-known to historians and civilians for many centuries.

As stated above, Osman was born as the son of a chief in northwestern Anatolia, in the town of Söguk sometime around the middle of the 13th century. The exact year has not been confirmed by any reliable sources, but 1258 is usually mentioned as most likely. His mother is presumed to be Halime Hatun, but even this has not been securely confirmed, and hardly anything is recorded of who she was. We know safely that Osman grew up in his hometown with two brothers but until his marriage to Mal Hatun there's not much information of his whereabouts. As the firstborn son of a local chief, Osman was aware of the fact that he would someday inherit the position, and it is said he learned to ride and fight already as a child. The first story recorded by the 15th-century historians of the Ottoman Empire is the one about how Osman became a Muslim. It was during a visit at his good friend Sheik Edebali's house, who was a very religious man, that he found the Quran. Osman became interested and asked his friend what this book was. His friend, who was an influential religious man in the community told him it was the holy book of Islam.

Osman lay awake that night, reading and reading until he couldn't keep his eyes open anymore. He fell asleep at the auspicious hour of dawn and then dreamed of a tree, sprouting from his navel with branches reaching all over the world. People in the dream were happy and the landscape was beautiful. When he woke up in the morning he told Edebali about the strange dream who in turn explained that because Osman had read the book so intensely and honestly, God had chosen him and his descendants to be blessed with glory and honor for many generations to come. Sheikh Edebali then gladly gave Osman his daughter Mal Sultana to marry and of their love, many poems have been written. The union of the two families benefited Osman greatly according to later sources because Sheikh Edebali was associated with very devout and ascetic dervishes. Though the dervishes didn't have any riches or power, their relationship to Allah would help benefit the Ottoman dynasty. The story of how Osman was the first in the family to actually become a devout Muslim was important to legitimize him taking over the remnants of the Seljuk Empire.

Osman's dream wasn't written down until almost 200 years later, a time when such a story would be of importance to keep the Ottoman Empire united. The story was valuable to the unification of separate Muslim emirates and gave Osman the right to conquer them. Another tradition that bears Osman's name is the girding of the sword of Islam given to him by his father-in-law. All sultans of the Ottoman Empire was girt with a ceremonial sword within two weeks of their accession to the throne, although not the same sword as Osman received from Edebali. Again, this practice was only introduced when Islam already had emerged as the prevalent ideology of the Ottoman Empire long after Osman's death, and again, the ceremony was mainly used to inflate the religious importance of the dynasty.

The year after his marriage to Mal Sultana, which probably took room in 1280, Osman's father passed away and left the 23-year-old son in charge of the beylik. The timing was perfect for Osman to become a world-famous conqueror and founder of an empire. In the west, the Byzantine Empire was falling apart and many cities made easy targets for Osman's army. In the east, the Mongols were wreaking havoc, contributing to the decline of the Seljuk Empire, and forced many Turks to flee the territories under Mongol siege. A great many ghazi warriors and potential soldiers streamed into Osman's emirate and gladly joined him in his quest against the Byzantine Empire.

The tradition of Ghazi warriors has been compared with the idea of the crusades or jihad. The word means "to carry out a military expedition or raid" in Arabic, but some scholars also mean that it indicates that the ghazi warrior fought to spread Islam. This is another fact debated in modern research, and there are no contemporaneous sources confirming that Osman was fighting in the name of Islam or that he really was a devout Muslim. As stated, these implications were written down much later by religious history writers at a time when they wanted to portray the founder of the empire as God's chosen man. What is known about the ghazi warriors is that they most likely fought as mercenaries and hence changed sides to whoever could pay them at the moment. Whatever their reasons might have been, the ghazi warriors were important contributors to Osman's success. Osman also added the word ghazi to his name, as did eight of his successors. Whether all of them defined themselves as simply conquerors or as religious men, it is impossible to say. The adding of Ghazi to their name nonetheless indicated their expansionist intentions.

After Osman had gotten married and his father had passed away, he was a full-fledged leader of the beylik, with a strategically important territory and prosperous family ties through his marriage. The stream of warriors and refugees made Osman a ruler of more people than his father, and with more people, more lands were needed. To expand the cost of the Byzantine Empire was a logical solution, and it is estimated that he started his expansionist campaign in the year 1288. His first target was two nearby fortresses, Karacahisar and Eskişehir. A decade later, in 1299, he conquered the two larger towns of Yarhisar and Bilecik from the crumbling Byzantine Empire. He made Yarhisar the new capital of the beylik and declared independence from the Seljuk Empire.

By then, the central rule of the empire was weak and the popular sultan had been forced to flee the lands a couple of decades earlier. In his wake, there was chaos and no strong ruling power. The newly born independent state under Osman was organized as a strong central government on the same principles as the previous Sultanate of Rum. Though many people in the peripheries were opposed to Osman's rule, he quickly lightened the tax burden of his new citizens which assuaged them and changed the negative opinion of him. He needed to establish trust and loyalty amongst the people who are furthest from the capital to stabilize the borders, and the low tax strategy worked well. He was also the first chief in the area to mint his own coins which points to Osman's ambition of creating a larger organized political entity.

After the declaration of independence, Osman continued to expand both southwest and north into Byzantine territory aiming to control the whole area between the Sea of Marmara and the Black Sea. He conquered towns along the coasts and the poorly organized Byzantine armies were coerced to draw back towards the Bosphorus. In 1308 he captured the last city on the Aegean coast, Ephesus, and thus achieved his goals of dominating the region. His mounted forces used multiple creative military strategies for defeating the enemies around the countryside of Bithynia and fought in ever-surprising formations. During his last years in life, he also had good help from his sons, especially the oldest, the heir to the throne Orhan. After a whole life on the battlefields with his father, Orhan had learned and fully mastered the ideas behind Osman's tactics.

The last successful campaign of Osman was the siege of Bursa, though his son was left in charge and Osman himself didn't participate physically. Orhan showed tenacity and chose to lay siege to the city instead of attacking and conquer it forcefully. The siege was successful and the city surrendered after two of years under the threat of starvation. This was the last and most important victory of Osman I's expansion in Anatolia, not fully complete until the same year Osman died, 1326. After Bursa fell under Ottoman rule, other cities in the vicinity soon followed suit. It became the new capital under Orhan and an important staging ground against further expansion to the west.

It is difficult to separate the legends surrounding Osman from facts, and little is known about his earliest endeavors. Osman gained some interest from contemporaneous writers with the capture of Ephesus and that's the first time he is mentioned in historical records from his own time. From 1308 there are reliable sources about how and what he managed to achieve, and the second half of his life is less mysterious than the first half. Osman's conquests gained importance because his son and grandson continued his expansionist ambitions and at the same time incorporated religious tolerance and political stability in their rule. No one could at the time was able to foresee what the Ottoman Empire would grow to be, though people already in an early stage took refuge under Osman and preferred him to many other rulers. When the Seljuk Empire finally disintegrated and collapsed in 1308 Osman's prosperous lands was a capacious, natural escape from raiding Mongols. After his death at the age of 68 his son, Orhan continued the expansion far beyond what his father had dreamed.

A picture of the tomb of Osman

Expansion

By the time of Osman's death and Orhan's ascension to the throne, there are more reliable sources, to be found. It's possible to retell certain historical dates and happenings correctly but still, Orhan's reign is also somewhat glorified and exaggerated by the history writers. Orhan was probably born in the year 1281, as the only son to Osman I and his first wife, Malhun Hatun. Before Orhan conquered Bursa in 1326 not much is known of him. He was over 40 years old when Osman died and left him in command of the territories he had conquered, all of which he, together with his brother Alaeddin took good care of. Alaeddin was the second son of Osman, but born of his second wife Rabia Bala Hatun, a woman of Arabic descent. There are still some divisive opinions about which of the two brothers actually were the oldest, but their different personalities are usually seen as a natural explanation for their partition of duties. Orhan became the chief as appointed by their father and later he made Alaeddin the vizier. Orhan was a military man, who had spent much of his adult life campaigning throughout Anatolia with Osman while Alaeddin was calm, benevolent, pious and more passive, and had received management training in administration and business.

The affinity between them stands out as something of an oddity in the Ottoman family. As the empire grew so did also the hunger for power, and the brothers of succeeding generations fought hard to claim the throne. In later years, the death of a sultan was cause for civil war to break out, and having your competing brothers murdered in cold blood. Alaeddin and Orhan, on the other hand, shared the duties and collaborated to rule the beylik even though Orhan was the one officially sitting on the throne. The story of how the brothers decided to share the burden is more or less fabricated to shine a glorifying light on them. The noble Orhan offered the throne to his brother, who, just as noble, turned it down stating their father had wanted Orhan as his heir. Orhan asked Alaeddin to become his vizier, a title he invented there and which simply means "bearer of a burden." This indicates that the brothers felt the inherited burden of responsibility from their father's accomplishments. Alaeddin accepted the title and only asked for a small patch of land close to Bursa while Orhan kept the rest of the lands under his rule. The records tell of how Orhan often sought Alaeddin's advice on administering and managing both the civil and the military institutions of the state. Together they shaped a strongly centralized government that became significant for the Ottoman Empire and modernized both politics, economy and military during its existence.

Before Alaeddin died in 1331 or 1332, he made important contributions to Orhan's rule. In 1329 he suggested to standardize a monetary system all over the beylik, to choose an official costume or outfit for the Ottomans and to reorganize the army. Coins with Orhan's name was stamped in the same year, white became the official color of the modest clothing worn by government and military officials, and the army was divided into smaller squadrons. This initiative implies that before there probably hadn't been any similar way to organize the soldiers, though it would later become the standard. With smaller units each led by an officer it was possible applying more advanced tactics and strategies in field battles. This system is usually attributed to Alaeddin in Ottoman records, though its origins still are under debate. He also suggested forming an army which only was summoned in wartime, and hence could contribute to society in other ways during times of peace. This is largely how modern armies use their soldiers today, but the idea was new for the time. The first experiment failed under Orhan's rule, because the armies lacked military training when needed. In later generations, these armies came in very useful.

Orhan had gotten married a first time in 1299, which resulted in two or three sons. Two of them reached fame and many sources can confirm their lives and whereabouts. Suleyman Pasha was the oldest and intended heir to the throne. He helped his father expanding his emirate mostly to the west and north taking big chunks of the Byzantine lands. After Bursa fell under Ottoman rule, the Byzantine commander chose to side with Orhan and their forces joined together. Orhan's armies kept deprecating the west and northern coastlines around the sea of Marmara and Bosporus. The Byzantine Emperor Andronicus III would not yield without a fight and was determined to stop Orhan in his advances and regain some of the lost lands.

The Battle of Pelekanon in 1329 was the first time the Byzantine armies met the Ottoman forces. The clash ended with a shattering defeat for the attacking Byzantines, although their numbers were larger and they possessed more experience from battle than the Ottomans.

Contemporaneous sources explain the crushing win with the Byzantine spirit already being broken by the empire's civil struggles while the confidence of the arising Turks made them fight with more vigor and conviction.

The Battle of Pelekanon marks a significant turning point in the history of the region. The Byzantine Empire never again tried to reclaim the lost territories on the Asian side of Bosphorus and more or less left Nicea and Nicomedia to be besieged and later incorporated into Orhan's beylik. By 1340 Orhan had also annexed the beylik of Karasi which was the first time he had chosen to march towards Turkish neighbors. He did so because the chief had passed away and the two sons of the chief were currently warring against each other to claim the title. Many soldiers and civilians had already died when Orhan decided to intervene for the sake of peace. One of the brothers was killed and the other captured and Orhan now ruled four provinces. Most of the cities within the beylik were peaceful and many former Christians quickly embraced Islam without coercion. The region needed to be stabilized in order to build the strong state apparatus as the foundation of an empire. Orhan had put all of Bithynia and the northwestern corner of Anatolia under his control without much resistance from the population.

After his brother's death in the early 1330s, Orhan had help of his two eldest sons Suleyman and Murad in expanding the emirate. In 1341, the Byzantine Emperor Andronicus III died and left an 8-year-old successor on the throne. The following civil war created a golden opportunity for the Ottomans to march further into the declining empire and inflict some irreparable damage. The fall of the empire would take another hundred years of power struggles, but there was no way to restore it to its former glory. A six-year-long civil war broke out on the Balkans, and since peace reigned in Orhan's lands, he chose to head further west attempting to create an Ottoman road to Europe.

The Byzantine Grand Domestic John VI Kantakouzenos, who was also the young emperor's custodian and acting as regent, recognized Orhan's potential and formed an alliance with the Ottoman chief. He gave his daughter Theodora in marriage and then used Orhan's help to usurp the throne and become Emperor of Byzantine in 1347. In exchange, Orhan gained the right to plunder Thrace and he started raiding the area regularly through the peninsula of Gallipoli. His oldest son Suleyman took charge of the plundering as Orhan himself was growing older and weaker. The raiding was fruitful and the Ottomans gained both land and riches, while the Byzantine emperor let them. This attracted thousands of uprooted Turkmen to head west and join in Suleyman's expeditions. The emperor of Byzantine had not intended for the Ottomans to actually take possession of Thrace, but that was, of course, inevitable. After Suleyman made Gallipoli into a permanent base for his raiding parties across present-day Bulgaria it didn't take long until John VI was more or less forced to sign over the lands to Orhan's family, a very prestigious win. Constantinople was now surrounded by Ottoman territory, albeit still under Byzantine rule.

It was by the end of Orhan's life that his oldest son died in an accident, which took a toll on Orhan's spirit. He withdrew from power and his last years were spent living quietly in Bursa. Before he died, his youngest son whom he had with Theodora, Sehzade Halil, was kidnapped by pirates along the Aegean coast. It is unclear if they knew who they were kidnapping but when realizing, they took refuge in a Byzantine fortress in Phocaea. After finding this out, Orhan appealed to the co-emperor Andronikos IV to rescue his son and promised in return to call off debts and withdraw his support for the Kantakouzenos family. Andronikus agreed and laid siege to Phocaea, which ended in Orhan paying 30,000 ducats as a ransom for his son. Halil was released in 1359 and it was decided he would marry another Byzantine princess to strengthen the ties between the two dynasties. The imperial family hoped to see Halil as the rightful heir to the beylik since the older brother Suleyman had died.

Their expectations would soon turn into disappointment when Murad was appointed successor to the throne and not the teenager born by Theodora. Murad took over the title and started ruling the emirate after Orhan's death. Orhan was the longest living and ruling chief of all the Ottoman leaders and died in 1362 at the age of 80. Shortly after Orhan's death Murad even had his half-brother executed accused of challenging Murad for the throne. The 16-year-old had already gotten married and produced two young boys who were now left fatherless. This was perhaps the start of brotherly distrust between the heirs of the Ottoman empire. The first sultans had neglected to formulate an order of succession and it was not until a hundred years later they constituted laws. Hence the throne was up for grabs by any of the sons when a sultan died, although usually some sort of pre-agreement had been made between the generations. Out of sight from the dead father the avaricious sons almost made it a habit to challenge each other for the throne. After Murad had executed his little brother, many more were to follow his example.

Murad I, the First Sultan

Murad was now the undisputed ruler of Osman's beylik, and the first major conquest attributed to him was that of Adrianople, the third most important city of the Byzantine Empire. As more sources have been found in later year,s it is now debated when the conquest really took place, and even who actually conquered Adrianople. It has been the general consensus that Murad laid siege to the city in either 1361 or 1362, but newer research holds 1367 or 1371 as more likely. There's also a possibility that it was not Ottoman Turks who conquered the city but some other group of the roaming ghazi warriors. It is also debated regarding when Murad moved his capital from Bursa to Adrianople, the general opinion being that Murad captured the city in 1362, renamed it Erdine and made it the new capital in 1363. Other sources say that the city still belonged to Byzantium by 1366 and was conquered in the 1370s by Murad's second lieutenant Lala Sahin Pasa, who also administered the city for some time after. The same source claims that Murad himself actually didn't enter Erdine until 1377, when the Byzantine Emperor Andronikos IV needed his help in a civil war. Erdine was the military center of the Ottomans in the Balkans, but Bursa was considered the capital until the conquest of Constantinople and the rebuilding of it into a new capital.

Murad I

Murad transformed the beylik into a sultanate in 1383 and declared himself sultan. His right hand, the second lieutenant Lala Sahin Pasa, became the governor of the western province Rumeli while Murad remained in control over Anatolia. At this point, he also instituted an army, referred to as Janissaries, and a recruiting system called Devshirme. This was possible thanks to the reorganization of the military, a seed which was planted by his uncle Alaeddin some 50 years earlier. The Janissaries were an elite infantry loyal only to the sultan. Their mission was to protect only him and in battles they were always the closest to him, forming a human shield. Originally they consisted of non-Muslim slaves, mainly Christian boys from Byzantium. Jewish boys were not taken as soldiers and Muslims could not, by law, be enslaved. Murad had instituted a tax of one fifth on all the slaves taken in war, and the idea of only taking boys fit for fighting was called Devshirme, or blood tax. The slaves went through a very strict training, first learning to speak Turkish and practicing Ottoman traditions by living with a family chosen by the sultan. The boys also were forcibly converted to Islam, forbidden from wearing a beard and lived under monastic circumstances in celibacy. They were overseen by eunuchs and trained in special schools, enhancing their personal abilities. The main difference between these and other slaves was that they were being paid for their services. This served as a motivator and kept the soldiers loyal.

The Janissaries were at first a hated institution by the subjugated Christian minorities. Rather than having their sons taken away, it happened that the parents disfigured their children so as to make them weak and unsuitable for Devshirme. But the status of the Janissaries grew. They became men of high learning and an ascetic nature, favored by the sultan. As they grew in numbers, they also became very influential in the capital and their skills as warriors made them feared far beyond the borders of the empire. The Janissary corps was the first of its kind and a groundbreaking contributor to the success of Ottoman warfare. At the time of Murad's reign, they were fewer and less respected than what they would become at a later stage, though they were quite significant for the conquering of the Balkans.

Not just the conquest of Erdine but also many other historical details in Murad's life is widely debated by historians today. Though it is difficult to prove the consecutive order of certain events in the fast-growing sultanate, it is certain that his reign was a bloody and expansive period, followed by more of the same by his successor. During the 1370s his second lieutenant and trusted friend Lala Sahin Pasa crushed the Serbian armies in the battle of Maritsa though they were heavily outnumbered. Using superior strategies and a surprise night-time attack, the Serbs were close to being annihilated and their king killed in the campaign. Little remained of the Serbian Empire and the lands were easily taken over by the Ottomans. They then aimed north and started raiding Bulgaria's southern borders. The Bulgarian king more or less acquiesced to vassalage, something that the Serbians, Macedonians and some of the Greek rulers already had done, though the Ottomans kept deprecating their borders. After capturing both Sofia and Nis by the year 1386, Murad was forced to return to Anatolia to settle rising troubles in the home province. In his wake, the bitter rulers of the Balkans formed an alliance and went to war against the Ottoman forces. Two of the Bulgarian princes, along with the Serbian Prince Lazar and more allies from Kosovo, Macedonia and Bosnia won their first battle against the Ottomans and took back Nis in 1388. Murad quickly responded by launching new campaigns in his recently conquered territories which resulted in the Battle of Kosovo in 1389.

The Battle of Kosovo was the apogee of Murad's fighting in the Balkans and turned into a bloodbath with significant losses on both sides. It was in the midst of summer, June 1389, that the two foes met slightly north of modern-day Pristina in the open fields of Kosovo. Records of the actual battle itself are scarce, but historians have managed to reconstruct a likely chain of events thanks to written down strategies, numbers, and information from other, similar battles.

The Serbian and Turkish sources often contradict each other, and what modern history books retell about the events are based on the general assumption and what most likely is true. Murad arrived backed up by a neighboring beylik from Anatolia, and together they had mustered an army of nearly 40,000 men. The Serbian Prince Lazar had, together with allies from Kosovo and Bosnia, an army the size of 30,000 men. As some sources claim, it is also likely that the Knight Hospitaller from Croatia fought on the Serbian side, and anachronistic records state that the Serbian army was larger than Murad's. Murad had both his sons with him, Bayezid and Yakub, commanding one wing each.

Initially, it looked like the Serbs would prevail and the Ottoman forces conceded heavy losses during the first hours. However, in a frenzy of bloodthirst and revenge, Bayezid led his wing in a counterattack towards the knights, whose heavy armor became a hindrance for their retreat. Bayezid slaughtered a great number of the Serbian soldiers, and Prince Lazar's allied Vuc Brankovic from Kosovo fled the field trying to rescue as many men as possible. At this point, Prince Lazar had probably been captured or killed in the heat of the battle. At the end, there was not much left of either army, the Serbian Prince Lazar had died, and Sultan Murad had been killed. There are three common stories about how and when he was killed - either in battle by Lazar, by one of the 12 Serbian lords who broke through Ottoman lines, or by an assassin in his own tent after the battle was won. No matter which story is true, it resulted in the oldest son Bayezid strangling his brother Yakud on the spot, so as to be the sole heir to the throne. Hence he pursued in his father's footsteps, as his father had also started his reign by killing his brother.

After the war, the Serbs didn't have enough troops left to defend their territory. Bayezid sent for more armies from the east and within a short period of time, most of the principalities became Ottoman vassals.

Murad I had died at the age of 62, and his organs were buried in the battlefield in Kosovo, while his body was transported and buried in Bursa. His legacy included a lot more than just new lands, and apart from his military reorganization, he also created the council of ministers called Divan, over which the grand vizier presided. This became the ruling political entity in the sultanate. He united the smaller emirates into two larger provinces, Rumeli and Anatolia, each ruled by a strong provincial vizier. The military court was also Murad's doing, and he introduced a legal system. At the same time, he expanded the sultanate in Anatolia but even more to the west of the Bosphorus, to include most of the Balkans and Bulgaria. When he died he left the sultanate ready to rule for his son Bayezid.

Bayezid I

Bayezid I

It would seem as if much of the hard work already had been done by the time Bayezid came to power in the Ottoman Sultanate. The difficult first century of expanding and stabilizing the new state had passed, and many of the foundational institutions been formed by Murad and Orhan. The military and government had been efficiently organized and now Bayezid needed to emulate his predecessors. After the battle of Kosovo and the losses of thousands of soldiers, as well his father, Bayezid continued to raid the Balkans. He maintained the borders to the south and coerced the Albanian, Macedonian and Serbian princes into vassalage. By marrying the daughter of the deceased Prince Lazar, he established a new bond with her brother, the soon-to-be-despot Stefan Lazarevic. After endorsing Stefan he left him in charge of the Balkan territories and returned to Anatolia to settle unrest in his homelands.

In 1390 he managed to conquer six different beyliks to the north and east of his territory before the winter fell, the first time an Ottoman ruler had decided to annex Turkish lands. It was partially because of his skills as a warrior and because of his fiery temper he gained the nickname Yildirim, lightning bolt.

The annexation of the Anatolian lands didn't come without consequences. Both Turkmen loyal to the Ottoman dynasty and outside of their territories expressed dissatisfaction and Bayezid sought peace with the larger emirate Karaman in 1391. He had been using fatwas, declared by Islamic scholars, to justify the expansion into Muslim territories, but this was as far as he would come in Anatolia.

After the peace was negotiated, he turned north with some success but was in the end forced to return west were rumors of an uprising circulated. It was the Hungarian King Sigismund who had cajoled Bulgaria's Ivan Shishman, the king of one of the vassal states, and the Wallachian ruler Mircea the Old, into an anti-Ottoman coalition. News of the alliance reached Bayezid who, true to his nickname, acted swiftly and ruthlessly. The Bulgarian vassal took most of the hit from Bayezid, who recaptured the lands and beheaded Shishman while leaving the distant Hungarian King and Wallachia to be dealt with later. Bayezid had to hurry south to settle disputes and bickering between the Greek lords under his rule.

After a successful meeting in Serre in 1394, he had reinstated his power over his vassal states, and by a series of events also managed to extend his vassalage to include the city of Athens. The same year he also laid siege to the Byzantine capital Constantinople, which called for help from the Hungarian Kingdom. The siege lasted for eight years, and during most of it, Bayezid had to keep fighting on other frontiers of his sultanate.

One of the last major crusades was launched in 1396 by Pope Boniface IX. The timing was perfect for the European kingdoms to unite and form a strong threat to the Turks. The 100-year war between France and England was in a state of truce and King Richard II had just married Princess Isabella of France. Both the Brits and the Franks sent forces to join in the crusade, and so did Hungary, Bulgaria, Venice, Genoa, Croatia, Wallachia, the Holy Roman Empire and the Knights Hospitaller. It is estimated that both the Crusader forces and the Ottoman armies consisted of somewhere between 15,000–20 000 men each, but the sources all tell different stories. Some tell of armies the size of hundreds of thousands of men, and some say that the enemy force was at least twice the size of their own army. The details of the battle are questionable since historians on both sides wrote to please and aggrandize their own leaders. In fact, the actual participation of English soldiers has not been proven, and records of such an army being sent abroad at the time don't exist. Genoa and Venice were probably also more engaged in other areas under their rule, although they surely sent a smaller convoy to backup the crusaders. On the Ottoman side, numbers vary just as much, but the coalition of Serbs and Turkmen could probably be numbered to less than 20,000.

On arriving at Nicopolis on the river Danube, the crusaders laid siege to the Ottoman-controlled city. Their first mistake was not to bring any siege armaments, making any attempt to conquer the city with force futile. The crusader generals changed tactics and decided to block the exits and the port of the city with the intention of starving the citizens, and in such a way make them surrender. During the siege, there wasn't therefore much for the soldiers to do but to play games, drink wine and wait for Nicopolis to give in. When rumors of the approaching Ottoman armies reached Nicopolis the French marshal, Boucicaut threatened to cut off the ears of anyone talking about the Turkmen. He thought the rumors of approaching soldiers would deflate the morals of the troops. Hence, little did they expect that a lightning bolt was rapidly heading their way from Constantinople. When Bayezid and his Serbian ally Lazarevic were six hours away from the camp the crusaders were in the midst of a drunken dinner celebration. In stress and panic, they started executing some 1000 prisoners they had taken in the town of Rachowa, which would later add to the fury of Bayezid.

The French, Hungarian and Wallachian rulers drew a battle plan in all haste, but they couldn't agree on the details. Sending the foot soldiers in first would be an insult to the great French knights having to follow in the lead of peasants, and therefore they had to go first into battle. Sigismund argued that the Turkish vanguard was not worthy of the French knights and that his infantry should take the lead. In the end, the French lords had their will and a couple of hours later the knights rode out to face the Turkish forces. Thanks to a hill hiding the full strength of the Ottoman army, the knights once again underestimated its foes and rode straight into annihilation.

After that initial clash, the rest of the French troops threw themselves to the ground, pleading for their lives. Bayezid knew the value of French nobility, so he took them hostage and later set them free for large ransoms. King Sigismund and the Master of the Hospitallers were the only leaders able to flee, and Sigismund later accused the French of hubris and for putting pride ahead of tactics. The rest of the noblemen were taken prisoners and many of the surviving soldiers were executed as retribution of the 1,000 murdered civilians from Rachowa. After the carnage, the hostages were marched in chains all the way to Gallipoli, where they were kept in prison for two months while waiting for the news to reach Central Europe. The fleeing Sigismund had failed to negotiate the ransom for his allies since Bayezid knew the Hungarian assets were depleted. It took over a year and a half before the last generals and noblemen returned to their homes, and many of them had already died from battle wounds or poor conditions while captured.

While all this took place, Bayezid continued his siege of Constantinople half-heartedly but gave up after striking a compromise with the Emperor Manuel II. It was agreed that Bayezid should have veto in approving and confirming all the future Byzantine emperors. Bayezid left Constantinople, never to return west of Bosphorus again. There was unrest in his annexed territories in Anatolia where the newly arrived Central Asian conqueror Timur was in the midst of establishing a new Mongolian Empire. With Bayezid occupied the Balkans, Timur had managed to form a coalition of the Ottoman vassal states against their sultan. Bayezid rushed to meet him with a strong 85,000 man army consisting of Turks, Serbs, Albanians, Tartars, ghazis and janissaries and even Christians. However, the 140,000 Mongol-Turkish cavalry troops accompanied by 32 war elephants must have put some fear in the defending Ottoman allies.

Heavily outnumbered and tired from the long march, the battle couldn't have started any worse for Bayezid's armies. Two of his allied forces switched sides during the battle, and when a defeat became inevitable the Serbian troops escaped with the Ottoman Treasury and one of Bayezid's sons. Stefan Lazarevic urged Bayezid to flee, but Bayezid kept his position and continued fighting. After the battle had been lost, Bayezid was captured by the Timurids and died in prison a couple of months later. Some historians claim he was being abused while taken hostage and driven to suicide, while others claim the opposite. One of his sons, Mustafa Celebi, was also captured with him but was held in Samarkand until Timur's death in 1405.

Bayezid's death had devastating consequences for the Ottoman Sultanate. Except for Mustafa who was in prison, Bayezid had four more sons, all hungry to rule the sultanate. The youngest, Mehmed Celebi, was confirmed as a sultan by Timur, but his brothers refused to acknowledge his authority. The result would be a civil war known as the Ottoman Interregnum, which lasted for over a decade. During the years of fighting, Mustafa stayed hidden from his brothers, plotting to make his move for when they had defeated each other.

The Ottoman Interregnum

Timur had no intentions of conquering or ruling Anatolia, and after he had won the Battle of Ankara he withdrew from the territory, satisfied with leaving the beyliks divided. The Ottoman family got to keep their lands around Bursa, and no one had made any claim to their acquisitions in the Balkans. The commotion gave a window opportunity for Thessaloniki, Kosovo, and Macedonia to break free from the vassalage, but the other states remained under Ottoman rule, awaiting the next sultan. The only significant losses of the dynasty after the war were pride and the trust of their Muslim neighbors whom they had annexed and ruled.

If Bayezid had not died in prison, the damage done to his sultanate by Timur would have been easy to repair. However, Bayezid had had many sons, and there was no set order of succession within the dynasty. The eldest son had died before the Battle of Ankara, and the next in age, Mustafa, was in prison in Samarkand. Four more sons thus had potential claims to the throne, although the youngest, Mehmed, had been recognized as the new sultan by Timur before he left. Naturally, the three others opposed this appointment of their little brother, and it didn't take long before war was raging between the four of them. The ensuing civil war lasted for 11 violent years.

The sources describing what led up to and finally caused the Interregnum reveal many different storylines about Bayezid and all his sons. He himself is said to have been tortured and compelled to commit suicide in the care of Timur, while one of his wives too was abused. It is said that Mustafa was not taken captive, but mysteriously vanished during the battle and it is also said that Isa and Musa escaped by themselves, while Suleyman and Mehmed were taken care of by Bayezid's allies. Other sources tell of both Musa and Mustafa being captured, with Musa being released after Mehmed's negotiations with Timur and Mustafa when Timur himself died. The order of the brother's ages is also not fully clear, nor is how they were allied with each other during the Interregnum. The general assessment is that three of the brothers each occupied different territories in the former United Ottoman Sultanate. The oldest, Suleyman, moved to the Balkans and established his capital in Erdine. Constantinople was still the capital of the Byzantine Empire, but the lands around it were occupied by Isa, one of the middle brothers. The youngest, Mehmed, took possession of the eastern parts and tried to strike a deal to share the Anatolian territories with Isa, who promptly refused and instead signed a treaty of friendship with the Byzantine emperor. The fourth brother Musa was probably in captivity for one year until Mehmed negotiated his release. Musa then aimed for Bursa, with the aid of Mehmed, and therefore contested the territories already ruled by Isa. It was not hard for Isa to defeat Musa in one of the earliest battles of the civil war, and Musa fled to Germiyanid in Mehmed's kingdom.

Next in line stood Mehmed, with a large army from eastern Anatolia. Mehmed and Isa met in the Battle of Ulubad in 1403. The battle ended in victory for Mehmed, who proclaimed himself King of Anatolia and again united the province under one rule. Isa fled to his allies in Constantinople and later moved even further west to form a coalition with his brother Suleyman. Suleyman took the opportunity to back Isa up and sent him back to Anatolia with a large army. To no avail, Mehmed won once again, and the subsequent fate of Isa is still disputed. Some say he went into hiding, while others say he was spotted in a Turkish bath and killed by Mehmed's agents in 1406. This is usually the year considered as the year of his death.

The belligerent state between the brothers was prodded on by the surrounding entities. Other emirs, the roaming ghazis, the Byzantine Empire, the Italian city-states, and the influential upper class of Bursa all had an interest in keeping the conflict going and weakening the political, economical and geographical stability in the territories. Mehmed gained some support because he was the youngest and hence considered less dangerous than his brothers.

Suleyman, who had been sitting comfortably on his throne in Erdine, together with his Grand Vizier Candali Ali Pashar and the support of Byzantine ruler John VII Palaiologos, started worrying about his brother's accomplishments in Anatolia and decided to take action. He marched on Bursa as well as Ankara and managed to conquer them both. While Suleyman was resting and regrouping in Bursa, Mehmed and Musa formed an alliance. By sending Musa through Wallachia to Suleyman's western borders, the eldest brother suddenly had a war on two fronts on his hands. The eldest brother was overwhelmed and decided to withdraw to fight for his territories in Rumeli. With the support of both Byzantium and also the Serb Stefan Lazarevic, he defended Rumeli and took to ruling his province from Erdine without further involvements in Anatolia.

Suleyman was not an able king though and took no interest in state affairs. After his grand vizier passed away, Rumeli fell into neglect and Suleyman's flamboyant lifestyle caused him to lose support among his allies and subordinates. When the bellicose Musa came for Erdine,

Suleyman had very few supporters left and the capital was easily conquered by the younger brother. Trying to escape to Byzantine lands, Suleyman was killed in 1411.

At this point, Musa and Mehmed co-ruled the Ottoman provinces between them, as had been done during the reign of Murad I. Even so, the brothers had no natural affinity for each other. Musa considered himself the sultan of Rumeli, while Mehmed considered him his vassal. This inevitably caused complications and the peace didn't last long. Musa had laid siege to Constantinople as a retribution for the Byzantine's support of Suleyman, and with the stirring conflict between the two remaining brothers, the emperor turned to Mehmed for help. Mehmed betrayed his brother and formed an alliance with Emperor Manuel II Palaiologos.

Meanwhile, Musa had support from many of his vassal states, along with Stefan Lazarevic, and the initial battles ended in Musa's favor. It wasn't until Lazarevic switched sides and Mehmed gained support from more Turkish emirs that Musa finally could be defeated and killed in the Battle of Camurlu in 1413. This left Mehmed as the sole survivor of the fighting brothers, and he could crown himself Sultan Mehmed I of both Anatolia and Rumeli. That put an end to the Ottoman Interregnum.

Mehmed I

After the fighting was over, Mustafa, the brother in hiding, decided to emerge and play his part in the Ottoman history. Backed up by the Byzantine emperor, whose ever-changing sympathies now had turned against Sultan Mehmed, together with the old Wallachian vassal Mircea, he demanded Mehmed cede half the sultanate to him. Mehmed denied the request and defeated Mustafa quite easily in battle. Mustafa took refuge in Thessaloniki and the Byzantine emperor exiled him by request from Mehmed.

As fate had it, Mehmed's problems didn't end with the death and exile of all his brothers. The ever-conspiring Manuel II Palaiologos cajoled Mehmed's nephew to make a move against his uncle, but the plot was uncovered and the nephew was blinded for his betrayal.

After a few other uprisings and the constant hard work of keeping all his subordinates united peacefully, Mehmed died in 1421, after eight years as a sultan. By this time, it was evident that the empire had become too big for one ruler to govern, and that the threats arising on both frontiers would continue to destabilize the whole sultanate. The empire would need another reorganization to grow further, but the following sultan, Mehmed's son Murad, also was fully occupied with battles for most of his reign. Since Murad was only 16 when he ascended the throne, his uncle thought he would be an easy target to challenge. The Byzantine emperor released Mustafa from his exile under the pretense that he was the rightful heir to the throne. With the emperor's help, Mustafa also managed to conquer Rumeli and become sultan of the province, if only for a couple of years.

Though Murad was young, he was a capable soldier and general, trusted by his troops and allies. After being defeated in battle, Mustafa fled back and took refuge in Gallipoli, with Murat close behind. The sultan laid siege to the city, captured Mustafa, and had him hanged, an undignified way to be executed in the Ottoman tradition but justified by the disloyalty of Mustafa. The hanging was an exceptional act during Murad II's rule since he took great pride in his dynasty's chivalric forefathers. He studied old epic tales of noble caliphs and warriors, always acting in modesty and piety with a strong sense of justice. Murad traced his heritage back to the ghazi kings and modeled his own image on it. This was done to muster support for the reestablishment of a strong, unified empire with aims to expand in the name of Islam.

Murad II

Murad II became known as the Ghazi Sultan and was seen as not only defending Islam against the Christians but also as a defender of other, less powerful Muslim beys. Thus he gained support from Muslims both far and near. He turned his armies towards Venice, the Karamids, Serbia and finally Hungary – all of which he fought successfully. He renounced the throne to his 12-year-old son in 1444, tired of a life of fighting and pleased with his achievements.

The renunciation was, however, seen as a golden opportunity for the Hungarian Empire, together with Venice and the Holy Roman Empire, to again venture into Ottoman lands and reclaim the Balkans. The young Sultan Mehmed II realized his age and inexperience would be a disadvantage and called back his father to lead his armies. Murad II accepted unwillingly, more or less coerced, and took to fighting the Battle of Varna in the same year. Both armies suffered great casualties, and due to the extreme losses, Murad didn't realize he had won until some days after the battle. He continued his reign for seven more years, during which he won the Second Battle of Kosovo, secured the Balkan borders, fought and defeated Timur's son Shah Rokh, and also conquered the Karamanids. His last efforts as a ruler stabilized the region and also deterred the Christian armies from coming to any potential aid for Constantinople when his son would implement one of history's most famous and consequential sieges.

Mehmed II

The Fall of Constantinople

From the moment Mehmed finally succeeded to the Ottoman throne for good in 1451, he took no chance to be vulnerable. For instance, when Murad's widow arrived to congratulate him on his succession, Mehmed received her warmly, but when she returned to her harem she found that her infant son had been drowned in the bath.

That same year, Mehmed moved to secure his borders. He renewed his treaty with Brankovic, leader of Serbia, and created a three-year treaty with Hunyadi, regent of Hungary. He also confirmed a treaty with Venice that his father had made in 1446. All of this would also help further his designs on Constantinople, which the Ottomans had ample reason for coveting. Control of the Bosporus would be extremely advantageous, and control of the Byzantine territory would bring large financial benefits in the form of taxation to the Ottomans. The Ottomans even described the city as their "red apple", an expression for their ultimate aspiration.

Mehmed's attack would be the 13th attempt at conquest against Constantinople, and he intended to do it right. In 1451, he began to build a fortress on the Bosporus at the place where the channel was at its narrowest, opposite Sultan Bayezid's Anadolu Hisar castle. Between the two castles, the Ottomans now had complete control of the Bosporus, which provided them with an ideal base from which to attack Constantinople from the northeast. Emperor Constantine sent embassies to speak with the Ottomans, but they were executed on the spot. Every passing ship was inspected, and when one Venetian ship disobeyed, everyone was killed.

In 1453, Mehmed told his advisors that his empire was not safe as long as Constantinople remained in Christian hands. He began to gather an army in Thrace, and every Ottoman regiment, along with hordes of mercenaries, were recruited; all in all, there were 80,000 regular troops and 20,000 *bashi-bazouks* ("others"), though some historians estimate there were as many as 160,000 troops. Furthermore, the year before, a German engineer called Urban had offered to build the Ottomans a cannon that would blast any walls, so the Ottomans paid for and received the weapon three months later. They then demanded one twice the size and received it in January 1453. It was 27 feet long and 8 inches thick, with a muzzle that was 2.5 feet across, making it capable of shooting a ball some 1,300 pounds a distance of over a mile. 200 men helped the cannon make its journey south to the outside of Constantinople's walls, and their manpower was also needed for smoothing out the road and reinforcing bridges.

Fausto Zorano's painting, *Mehmet II conquering Constantinople*

Orthodox Easter 1453 was on the 1st of April, and on April 5th, Mehmed pitched a tent and sent a message to Constantine - one required under Islamic law - offering to spare all subjects in return for immediate surrender. He received no reply, so the cannon opened fire the next day. The people of Constantinople were not surprised, as they had worked in previous months on their city's defenses, but they were sorely lacking in resources. At their disposal, they had only eight Venetian vessels, five Genoese, and one vessel each from Ancona, Catalonia, and Provence. From the Byzantine Empire's own navy, there were only 10 vessels, meaning they only had 26 ships total. In terms of manpower, there were only 4,983 able-bodied Greeks and 2,000 foreigners, much too few to stand guard along 14 miles of wall, let alone face the 100,000 strong Ottoman army.

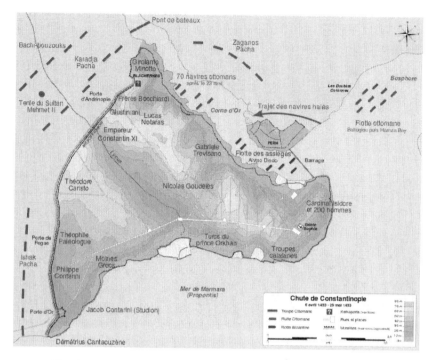

The siege lines, with the Ottomans in green and the Byzantines in red.

Nonetheless, all the defenders were in their places when the firing started. The emperor and Giovanni Giustiniani, the Genoese captain, were in command of the most vulnerable section, the area of the wall that crossed the valley of the little river Lycus about a mile from the northern end. The sea walls were less thoroughly manned than the land walls, but their garrisons also served as lookouts, reporting on the movements of the Turkish ships.

Despite these defenses, the Sultan was subjecting the land walls to a bombardment unprecedented in the history of siege warfare. By the evening of that first day, Mehmed II and the Ottoman troops had pulverized a section near the Charisius Gate, after which his soldiers tried to smash their way through, but it held. They went back to their camp at nightfall, and the Byzantines rebuilt it overnight.

Mehmed decided to hold his fire until he could bring reinforcements, and the bombardment resumed on April 11, continuing 48 more days uninterrupted. The larger cannon could only be fired once every two or three hours, but the damage was enormous, and within a week, the outer wall across the Lycus had collapsed in several places. The Byzantines worked ceaselessly to repair it, but the damage continued.

On April 20, ships from Genoa arrived off the Hellespont. Because Sultan Mehmed was determined to amass the strongest possible naval force outside Constantinople, he had left those straits unguarded, so the arriving ships were able to enter into the Marmara unhindered. As they arrived, the Sultan rode around the head of the Golden Horn to give the order personally to his admiral, Süleyman Baltoglu, that they were absolutely not to be allowed to reach the city. Baltoglu prepared to attack, but there was a strong southerly breeze, and his ships were unmanageable against the heavy swell. His overwhelmed captains were virtually defenseless against the deluge of arrows and javelins that greeted any approach, so they were forced to stand by as the ships sailed serenely toward the Golden Horn. When the wind dropped, Baltoglu gave the order to ram the Genoese ships and board them, but Turkish ships rode low in the water, so even when they successfully rammed the other vehicle, climbing into it was impossible. The Genoese sailors were also equipped with large axes and used them to take off the hands and heads of any who wished to enter. Ultimately, the Genoese captains lashed their ships together and were able to move toward the Horn as a giant floating fortress; a few hours later, in the middle of the night, they entered the city.

Sultan Mehmed II had watched every moment of the battle from land and was so furious with its outcome that he ordered Baltoglu's execution. The admiral avoided death after his subordinates testified to his courage, but he was nevertheless sent packing. The Sultan next set his sights on the Golden Horn. He had already put his engineers to work on a road running behind Galata, from the Marmara shore, over the hill near what is now Taksim Square, and down into the Horn itself. The engineers and laborers had cast iron wheels and metal tracks, and the carpenters were hard at work building wooden cradles that could hold the keels of moderate-sized vessels. It was a remarkable undertaking, and on Sunday, April 22, the Genoese colony in Galata watched with astonishment as 70 Turkish ships were hauled in by teams of oxen over the 200 foot hill and lowered into the Horn.

Fausto Zorano's painting, *Mehmed II at the siege of Constantinople*. This one depicts Ottoman troops transporting their fleet overland to the Golden Horn.

The Byzantines could not believe what was happening, and they no longer had a secure harbor, which also meant that they now had three and a half more miles of sea wall to defend, including the section breached by the Crusaders in 1204. Byzantine attempts to attack the Ottoman navy failed, while initial frontal assaults by the Ottomans also failed. Near the end of April, the defenders ostentatiously beheaded hundreds of Ottomans atop the walls as a sign for the invading army, but they would not be deterred. A Venetian in Constantinople at the time wrote in his diary, "They found the Turks coming right up under the walls and seeking battle, particularly the Janissaries...and when one or two of them were killed, at once more Turks came and took away the dead ones...without caring how near they came to the city walls. Our men shot at them with guns and crossbows, aiming at the Turk who was carrying away his dead countryman, and both of them would fall to the ground dead, and then there came other Turks and took them away, none fearing death, but being willing to let ten of themselves be killed rather than suffer the shame of leaving a single Turkish corpse by the walls."

Medieval depictions of the siege.

By the beginning of May, Constantine knew they would not hold out much longer; they were running out of food, and his troops were taking more and more time off of defending the city in order to find food for their families. His last faint hope was a promised Venetian relief mission, but he did not know whether it was actually on its way, what it held, or how big it was. He also did not know when it would come or how it would get through the Golden Horn, now that the Ottomans controlled it. He felt that his fate lay in the answers to these questions, so before midnight on May 3, a Venetian ship flying the Turkish flag and carrying a crew of 12 dressed in Turkish disguise slipped out.

Meanwhile, the Ottomans had given up on frontal attacks and were trying more traditional siege tactics, including tunneling under the walls to plant mines, not to mention the constant bombardment. The Byzantines dug counter-mines to locate and stop the Turkish tunnels, and they succeeded in destroying several Turkish attempts underground. Growing impatient, Mehmed sent a letter to Constantine on May 21 offering to let the people inside survive if they surrendered, and also letting Constantine head to the Peloponnese, which would be virtually the only remaining Byzantine possession. Constantine was willing to assent to the conditions, but not for the price of Constantinople, replying, "Giving you though the city depends neither on me nor on anyone else among its inhabitants; as we have all decided to die with our own free will and we shall not consider our lives."

However, two days later, when the secret Byzantine ship returned on May 23rd, its captain reported that they had combed the Aegean for weeks but had seen no trace of the promised Venetian relief expedition. Historian John Julius Norwich described the scene: "and so they had returned, knowing full well that they were unlikely to leave the city alive. Constantine thanked each one personally, his voice choked with tears."

There were also omens, or at least so they were interpreted by the Byzantines. On May 22 there was a lunar eclipse, and days later, as the holiest icon of the Virgin was being carried through the streets as an appeal to her intercession, it slipped from its platform. The morning after that, the city was shrouded in fog, which was unheard of at the end of May, and that same night the dome of St. Sophia was suffused with an unearthly red glow from the base to the summit, something that was even disturbing to Mehmed. His astrologers assured him that it was a sign that the building would soon be illuminated by the True Faith, and the Byzantines took it as a sign that the Spirit of God had deserted their city. Constantine's ministers begged him to leave the capital while there was still time and lead the empire from the Morea until he could recover the city. He fainted just as they spoke this suggestion; but when he recovered, he was determined as ever to not leave his people.

Meanwhile, the Sultan held a council of war on May 26, where he declared that the siege had continued long enough and that the time had come for a final assault. He announced that the following day would be filled with preparations, and the one after with rest and prayer, but they would begin the attack the morning of May 29, and they made no effort to conceal their plans from the Byzantines. They prepared for the next 36 hours without interruption, even lighting huge flares at night to help the soldiers with their labors. Then, at dawn on the 28th, they ceased. Mehmed set off on a day-long tour to inspect their preparations, finishing late in the evening and exhausted.

Inside the city, work on the city walls continued, but the people also gathered for one last collective appeal to God. Bells pealed, and the most sacred icons and precious relics were carried out to join a long spontaneous procession passing through the streets and along the whole length of the walls. They paused for special prayers where they expected the Ottoman artillery to concentrate particularly heavily. When the procession finished, the Emperor summoned his commanders and told his Greek subjects that there were four causes worth sacrificing one's life: his faith, his country, his family, and his sovereign. The Emperor told them they must be prepared to give their lives for all four tomorrow, and that he was prepared to sacrifice his own life. Next, he turned to the Italians and thanked them for their service. He told them that they and the Greeks were now one people, and that with God's help they would be victorious.

At dusk on the 28th, people from all over the city made their way to the Church of Holy

Wisdom - St. Sophia, the spiritual center of Byzantium - for the last service of vespers ever to be held in it. Virtually every man, woman and child who was not on duty that evening gathered in the Hagia Sophia to take the Eucharist and pray for deliverance. The Emperor arrived and asked for forgiveness for his sins from every bishop present, both Catholic and Orthodox, and then took communion. Later, after all the candles were out and the church was entirely dark, he spent time in prayer before returning home for a last farewell to his household. Around midnight, he rode the length of the land walls to assure himself that everything was ready.

Picture of the Hagia Sophia taken by Arild Vågen

Mehmed gave his signal at 1:30 in the morning on the 29th, and suddenly the silence was shattered. The Turks made their advance known with blasts of trumpets, hammering of drums, and bloodcurdling war cries. The Byzantine church bells pealed in response. The final battle had begun.

Mehmed knew that to succeed, he could not allow the Byzantines any rest. He first sent forward his mercenary soldiers, the *bashi-bazouks*, who were poorly armed and poorly trained, but they commanded some terrifying initial force. They flung themselves against the walls for two hours. Then, shortly before four in the morning, Mehmed called for the second wave of the attack, made by several regiments of Anatolian Turks who were significantly better trained and disciplined. They nearly forced entry, but the defenders - led by the Emperor himself - closed around them, killed many, and forced them back.

Mehmed determined that victory must be won not by the Anatolians but by his very own elite regiment of Janissaries. He next sent them into battle, offering the Byzantines no time to rest. The Ottoman troops advanced swiftly across the plain, hurling themselves at the stockades and hacking away at the supports. They also put up scaling-ladders to climb the walls. Instead of attempting to use them, however, these Janissaries had the opportunity to alternate with a fourth round of troops and rest while they waited for their next turn. The defenders, short-handed and exhausted, had no opportunity. They could not last much longer, but the walls still hadn't given way.

As if the defenders didn't have enough problems, they were struck with bad luck literally when shortly after dawn, Giovanni Giustiniani, the Genoese general who had been guarding the wall's weakest point with the emperor, was struck by lightning. In excruciating pain, he was carried to a Genoese ship in the harbor, but before the gate could be relocked, Mehmed saw the opening and sent in another wave of Janissaries. They forced the Greeks to retreat to the inner wall, and once they were caught between the two rows of walls, they were trapped and highly vulnerable. Many were slaughtered in place.

A short distance to the north, both sides could see a Turkish flag now flying over a tower. An hour before the slaughter between the fortifications, a group of Turkish mercenaries had found a small door, half-hidden at the foot of a tower, that was unlocked. It was a sally-port through which the Genoese had executed several effective raids on the Turkish camp, but now the *bashi-bazouks* mercenaries managed to force it open and make their way to the top of the tower. They hoisted their flag, left the door open for others to follow, and Turkish regiments poured in through all the open breaches. Emperor Constantine plunged right into the fray and was never seen again.

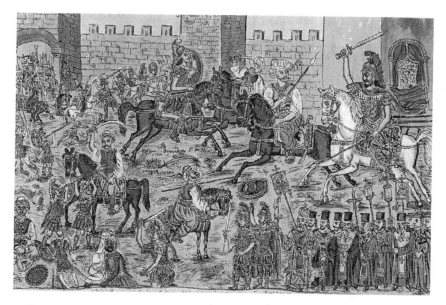

Theophilos Hatzimihail's depiction of fighting inside Constantinople. Constantine is depicted on the white horse.

By early morning, there were scarcely any living defenders. All the surviving Greeks had raced home to try to protect their families from the Ottomans' raping and pillaging, the Venetians were racing to the harbor, and the Genoese were trusting in the relative security of Galata. The Genoese found the Horn by and large quiet, while the Venetians had no trouble getting out of the harbor, into the Marmara, and out to the open sea.

As was often the custom in the Middle Ages, the Ottomans were ruthless in their ransacking. By noon, the streets were full of running blood, women and children were raped or stabbed, and churches, icons, and books were destroyed. The Empire's holiest icon, the virgin Hodegetria, was hacked into four pieces and destroyed. One writer said that blood flowed in the city "like rainwater in the gutters after a sudden storm", and that the bodies of both Turks and Byzantines floated in the sea "like melons along a canal".

The worst massacre was at the Hagia Sophia, where services were underway when the Turks began attempting to raze the church. The Christians shut the great bronze doors, but the Turks smashed their way in. The congregation was all either massacred on the spot or carted away to a Turkish prison camp. The priests tried to continue with mass until they were killed at the altar. Some Christians believe that a few of them managed to grab the patens and chalices and disappear in to the southern wall of the sanctuary, to wait until the city became a Christian city again, at which time they would resume the service right where it was left off.

Sultan Mehmed had promised his soldiers the traditional three days of looting, but by evening there was nothing left, and he called it off to little protest.

The historian and administrator Tursun Bey provided the sole detailed contemporary account of the siege in the Ottoman language:

> "Once the cloud of smoke of Greek fire and the soul of the Fire-worshipping Prince had descended over the castle 'as though a shadow,' the import was manifest: the devout Sultan of good fortune had, as it were, 'suspended the mountain' over this people of polytheism and destruction like the Lord God himself. Thus, both from within and without, [the shot of] the cannons and muskets and falconets and small arrows and arrows and crossbows spewed and flung out a profusion of drops of Pharaonic-seeming perspiration as in the rains of April - like a messenger of the prayers of the righteous - and a veritable precipitation and downpouring of calamities from the heavens as decreed by God. And, from the furthest reaches below to the top-most parts, and from the upper heights down to ground level, hand-to-hand combat and charging was being joined with a clashing and plunging of arms and hooked pikes and halberds in the breaches amidst the ruin wrought by the cannon.

On the outside the Champions of Islam and on the inside the wayward ones,

pike to pike in true combat, hand-to-hand;

Now advancing now feinting, guns [firing] and arms drawn,

Countless heads were severed from their trunks;

Expelling the smoke of the Greek fire, a veritable cloud

of sparks was rained on the Champions of Islam by the infidels;

Ramming into the castle walls, the trenches in this manner,

They set off the Greek fire, the enemies;

[In turn] they presented to the bastion their hooked pikes,

Drawn, they were knocking to the ground the engaged warriors,

As if struck in the deepest bedrock by the digging of a tunnel

It seemed that in places the castle had been pierced from below.

By the early part of the forenoon, the frenzy of the fiery tumult and the dust of strife had died away."

Fausto Zorano's painting, *Mehmed II, Entering to Constantinople*

George Sphrantzes, who was in Constantinople when it fell, wrote about the aftermath: "On the third day after the fall of our city, the Sultan celebrated his victory with a great, joyful triumph. He issued a proclamation: the citizens of all ages who had managed to escape detection were to leave their hiding places throughout the city and come out into the open, as they were remain free and no question would be asked. He further declared the restoration of houses and property to those who had abandoned our city before the siege, if they returned home, they would be treated according to their rank and religion, as if nothing had changed."

Perhaps most notably, after the siege was complete, Mehmed, Tursun Bey, the empire's chief ministers, imams, and the Janissaries rode to the Hagia Sophia. Mehmed picked up a handful of earth and sprinkled it over his turban as he entered as a gesture of humility, and as he approached the altar, he stopped one of the soldiers he saw hacking at the building's marble and informed him that looting did not apply to public buildings. He then commanded the senior imam to ascend to the altar and proclaim the name of Allah. With nothing more than the removal of Christian paraphernalia and their replacement with Muslim pulpits and minarets, the legendary Hagia Sophia became a mosque. The simplicity of the transformation was at once delicate and brutal, as evidenced by the way it's referred to among the Western world and the Turks. In the Christian world, the events are known as "the Fall", but for the Ottomans of history and the Turks of today, it was and remains "the Conquest."

For the Byzantine Empire, losing its beloved capital was the final nail in the coffin, and it didn't take long until the last refuge, Morea on the Peloponnese, was annexed and incorporated by Mehmed. The empire had managed to stay alive for over a thousand years, but after the belligerent rise of the Ottoman Empire, the past century had overwhelmed its rulers. Internal and external conflicts brought the empire to its knees, and the strong unification of the Turkish tribes proved to be a worthy successor of the empire. After the last emperor died without any heirs, all of his nephews were taken into palace service at Mehmed's court. As the two families had many intermarriages and alliances during the years, the boys quickly adapted to life under the Ottoman rule, were converted to Islam, and rose in the ranks of the sultanate. The youngest nephew later became the grand vizier to Mehmed's son and heir, Bayezid II.

The rise of the Ottoman Empire was possible thanks to the weakened state of their long-lasting foe, the Byzantine Empire, but also due to the power vacuum left by the Seljuk Empire. The empire was perfectly located, with more or less direct access to both Europe and Asia, yet still far away from the raiding Mongols. The conditions paved the way for determined leaders like Osman and his son Orhan to unite and stabilize the area, while at the same time expand the borders. Whether or not Osman was a Muslim, his successors were, giving incentive to battle and conquer the Christian Balkans, as well as annex other Muslim emirates. The dream of Osman became an important image through the centuries. Like the tree branches in the dream spread all over the world, so would Islam under the Ottoman rule.

Learning from mistakes made by previously fallen empires, the Ottomans set out to create a strong, centralized state, with efficient governance, large armies, and prospering cities. During the rise of the empire, they were careful not to rule with terror, but with pragmatism and reason. They were wise enough to let science and religion grow side by side, as well as earthly and heavenly riches. This drew interest from Muslims and Jews living under poor conditions in other kingdoms, and it attracted scholars, theologians, artists, and scientists, contributing to a flourishing culture in Anatolia.

When Constantinople was conquered and the Byzantine Empire finally fell, the Golden Age of the Ottoman Empire began. Mehmed II started by rebuilding and repopulating Constantinople, while also encouraging the Greeks and Genoese who had fled the city to move back into the trade quarters so vital to the city. He guaranteed safety to anyone willing to return and demanded that a mix of Christians, Jews, and Muslims populate the city. He restored the Orthodox Patriarchate, instituted a Jewish Grand Rabbinate, and ensured that within 50 years, Constantinople was again the most thriving city in the region, only now as the capital of the Ottoman Empire.

Although he spent so much time on the battlefields, Mehmed II's legacy includes a great improvement of the state apparatus, the rebuilding of Constantinople, and the intellectual renaissance of Anatolia. After the conquest of his future capital, the leftovers from Byzantium had to be swept up by a suitable ruler. Between his cultural and social transformations in the empire, he also had time to conquer more lands than any of his predecessors. In Europe, he was known as the Bloodthirsty, while in his homelands he was considered a hero.

For the Ottoman Empire, the Golden Age had just begun, and the empire's end would not come for nearly another 500 years.

The Tanzimat and Reforms

The Tanzimat (1839 -1876) was a series of reforms implemented across the empire and in various areas meant to modernize the Ottoman Empire and put an end to the Empire's economic, political and military stagnation. After the defeat at the battle of Vienna in 1683, along with the earlier naval defeat of Lepanto in 1571, the Ottoman Empire indeed entered almost two hundred years of stagnation. During this time some of its conquests were rolled back by European powers, along with Russia. At the end of the War of the Holy League (1683-1699), which ended with the signing of the Treaty of Karlowitz in 1699, the empire ceded most of Hungary and other smaller possessions in central Europe, as well as Dalmatia along the Adriatic Sea and the Peloponnese peninsula in Greece, later reconquered. During the same time, it was faced with the first series of wars with Russia, as the new Tsar, Peter the Great implemented a new policy of "access to the sea." This prevented the Ottoman's Crimean allies, who usually sent cavalry reinforcements to fight alongside regular Ottoman troops, from supporting Ottoman forces in central Europe. Despite several Russian defeats, the conflict ended with the capture of Azov, the Ottoman's stronghold in Crimea in 1696, and was a sign of the growing threat Russia posed to the Ottomans. Russia increasingly saw the Ottoman Empire as its objective rival in its quest to assert control over the Black Sea. After the initial capture of Azov, which was also seen as the birth of the Russian Imperial Navy, Russia continuously defeated the Ottomans. This was particularly the case after it finally defeated its previous rival, Sweden, in 1718, and was able to focus its military resources against the Ottomans.

This period also saw the *Yeni Ceri* ("New Soldiers" or *Janissaries*) win their war of influence against the Ottoman nobility. There was a natural rivalry between the Turkish nobility who formed the Ottomans' cavalry (the *Sipahis*), and the Janissaries, the Ottoman foot soldiers who were initially foreign slaves coming from Christian villages under Ottoman occupation. This rivalry, also largely fueled by the Sultan who saw it as a way to prevent both sides from allying against him, turned in the Janissaries' favor during the mid-sixteenth century, leading to the confiscation of the Sipahis' lands, and the consolidation of their power. The Janissaries would from this point grow to be a burden to the Ottoman Empire. They rose in numbers from 17,000 Janissaries in 1648 to an estimated 135,000 in 1826,[2] and were notoriously corrupt. More importantly, they acted against any attempt to reform the Ottoman military.

In 1807, the Sultan decided to replace them with a new modernized infantry as part of the *Nizam-ı Cedid* or "New Order" military reform. The reform was in response to the military defeats suffered during Napoleon's invasion of Egypt and the Ottomans defeat during the Russo-Turkish war (1787-1792). In their last successful uprising after receiving the support of Shaykh ul Islam (grand scholar of the Ottoman Empire), the Janissaries deposed the initiator of the reforms, Sultan Selim III, and disbanded the European-styled *Nizam-ı Cedid* army in 1807. In 1825, however, Sultan Mahmud II issued a fatwa stating that it was the duty of every Muslim to serve in the Ottoman military while reinstating the *Nizam-ı Cedid Army* in 1826, in an attempt to replace the Janissaries. When the Janissaries revolted in 1826 and sacked parts of Constantinople, the Sultan crushed the revolt, leading to the death of 4,000 Janissaries, and the subsequent dismantling of the old military force. This failed revolt, also known as the "Auspicious Incident" opened the way for broader military and political reforms, the *Tanzimat*.

On November 3, 1839, four months after the death of Sultan Mahmud II, who laid the groundwork for such reforms, Sultan Abdulmecid I issued the *Hatt- I Serif of Gulhane* ("Noble Edict of the Rose Chamber"). The document called for sweeping reforms within the Ottoman Empire, taking on ideas developed previously regarding the building of an Ottoman State that would guarantee security, property and equity among all subjects of the empire regardless of their religion or race. The decree promised to protect the lives and properties of its subjects, insert a new code of Justice asserting equal status of Muslims, Jews and Christians before the law, create a regular tax system and develop a just conscription method for service in a modernized army and navy. It effectively undermined and almost ended the system of the *millet,* where each religious group (millet) had officials responsible for tax collection, education, justice as well as religious affairs.

---

[2] George F. Nafziger (2001), Historical Dictionary of the Napoleonic Era

Sultan Mahmud II

Sultan Abdulmecid I

The first wave of reforms was led by Mustafa Reshid Pasha, who would be six times Grand Vizier and twice Foreign Minister between 1839 and 1858. Prior to the Edict, he had been the Ottoman Ambassador in France and later its Foreign Minister and came to be known as the "Father of the Tanzimat."[3] One of the first Ottoman bureaucrats to receive a European education, Pasha had traveled through much of Europe and developed friendly relations with French and British statesmen. However, while Western principles were the major source of inspiration for *Hatt- I Serif of Gulhane*, the document itself made a notable effort to place the reforms in the context of the Ottomans Islamic heritage. In fact, it started by placing the Islamic law (*Sharia* or *Şeriat*) as a central source of inspiration, and alleging that the Empire's decline was due to its lack of observance of the *Şeriat*: "All the world knows that since the first days of the Ottoman State, the lofty principles of the Qu'ran and the rules of the *Şeriat* were always perfectly observed. Our mighty Sultanate reached the highest degree of strength and power, and all its subjects [the highest degree] of ease and prosperity. But in the last one hundred and fifty years,

---

[3] Shaw and Shaw, History of the Ottoman Empire

because of a succession of difficulties and diverse causes, the sacred Şeriat was not obeyed nor were the beneficent regulations followed; consequently, the former strength and prosperity have changed into weakness and poverty. It is evident that countries not governed by the laws of the Şeriat cannot survive."[4]

Pasha

The Edict could thus be seen as an attempt to find the roots of the upcoming reforms in the Islamic principles, and reconcile the Ottoman heritage with the European reforms in the same way Japan adopted the *Wakon-yosai* ("Japanese spirit, Western techniques") as a slogan for the modernisation of the country. However, many of the reforms that followed and were portrayed as being rooted in the Islamic heritage did in fact go against much of the rules of the Sharia. The Tanzimat's second major Edict, the *Islâhat Hatt-i Humayun* or Imperial Rescript in 1856, made no mention of the Islamic heritage, and the increasing adoption of the Napoleonic Codes during

---

[4] Akram Fouad Khater, Sources in the History of the Modern Middle East, Cengage Learning 8 January 2010

the whole period clearly undercut this initial narrative. The acceptance of both European law and bureaucracy was a radical departure from the traditional "Din ve Devlet" principle that governed the Ottoman state until then, and regarded the faith (Din) and the state (Devlet) as a single institution.

The Edict of Gulhane was followed by a series of economic, social, political and military reforms. On the economic level the Edict led to a series of reforms meant to liberalize the economy and move away from state interventionism and protectionism. This was done by cancelling archaic measures or entities such as the *Iltizam* (tax-farming) or the various guilds. New concepts were introduced including the first Ottoman banknote in 1840, new banks, along with new European laws to regulate free trade, namely the Napoleonic Trade Laws. These economic reforms and the influx of foreign investment and loans contributed to an unprecedented boom in the building of infrastructure, including roads, ports and other major ways of commerce and transport. However, they were also largely indebted to the Ottoman state, encouraged by France and Britain, which were experiencing incredible financial development. European banks began funneling savings into overseas loans, which in turn encouraged their respective governments to facilitate the taking of loans by their Eastern ally. In 1854, the Empire first entered into loan contracts with European creditors in a move that ended with the Decree of Ramadan, the Ottoman default on its sovereign debt, on October 30, 1875.

Socially, the Edict expanded and consolidated the Ottoman bureaucracy to create a new tax system as well as a legal and military administration, enabling the apparition of a new Ottoman elite. In 1846, a plan for state education was implemented, including the creation of a system of primary and secondary schools leading to university, under a Ministry of Education. The limited budget devoted to the creation of these schools, however, hindered the realization of these reforms. Despite that, these changes were significant. They explained the difference between the previous reforms under Selim III, which were driven by the Sultan, and those undertaken during the Tanzimat, spearheaded by a new generation of Ottoman bureaucrats also known as the "Men of the Tanzimat" (*Tanzimatçılar*). The creation of a newly, westernized bureaucracy reinvigorated the wave of reforms later, at a time when it was under growing strain and opposition from within. Ottoman intellectuals, such as the Young Ottomans (see the First Constitutional Era), the Young Turks or even the followers of Mustafa Kemal and Mustafa Kemal himself, all came from that new class of bureaucrats whose purpose was to reform and save the Empire.

On the military level, the first period of reforms was marked by the introduction of conscription along with a fixed period of military service introduced in 1843 and based on the Prussian Conscription Law of 1814. The Ottoman military was then divided into five Imperial Armies garrisoned in different regions of the Empire. The military service was established as a period of five years between the ages of 20 to 25 along with an additional seven years of reserve duties. The first and second military reforms also saw the emergence of a new, more educated class of middle to high ranking officers and cadets, who progressively became involved in the Ottoman palace politics, as illustrated by the May 1876 coup (see the First Constitutional Era).

The second wave of reforms started with the *Islâhat Hatt-i Humayun* or Imperial Rescript issued on February 18, 1856. The decree was largely inspired by proposals made by France and Britain who assisted the Ottoman Empire during the Crimean war (1853-1856) against Russia. Both Britain and France used their status as allies to encourage further Westernization of the Empire, as the impact of the initial wave of reform was seen as limited. The second wave of reform was also partly the result of some frustration among the Ottomans regarding the limited results of the initial reforms, which introduced a series of new concepts, yet were either hardly implemented as a whole, or had only an impact on the most central areas of the Empire.

The decree affirmed more clearly the equality of all subjects of the Empire without distinction of race or religion, thus largely expanding the scope of the previous edict. It also differed by creating a new political mechanism that, to a certain extent, limited the power of the Sultan. The Sultan, for instance, promised to be held accountable for the creation of Provincial and Communal Councils. The decree further led to the creation of the Ottoman Penal Code in 1858 based on the Napoleonic code of 1810, further consolidating what was already achieved during the first wave of reforms. The code resulted in the establishment of a secular penal system, along with a system of courts that included tribunals of first instance, courts of appeals and a high court of appeal. As significant was the implementation of an educational plan dubbed the Regulation of Public Instruction in 1869, based on the principle of free compulsory education mentioned in the *Islâhat Hatt-i Humayun*.

During this second wave of reforms, the Ottoman Empire also reorganized its provinces under the "Vilayet Law" of 1864. The Vilayet Law replaced the Eyalet system, which divided the Empire into provinces by further subdividing each province into much smaller administrative units, while creating a new bureaucratic hierarchy for each of the administrative units created and expanding their power. The law was aimed at both asserting the central authority of the state over its provinces while also delegating more authority to these local governors. However, its interpretation by local governors, and the lack of qualified men to take these positions proved problematic. While the Ottoman elite was growing more educated, it reluctantly left Constantinople and the heart of the Empire. The decentralized powers of the governors and other smaller administrators would also be used against the integrity of the Ottoman Empire as France and Britain carved their own areas of influence within the Empire.

The First Constitutional Era

The two waves of reforms triggered different sorts of opposition. One of the most common and probably the strongest in terms of sheer number was the one stemming from conservative elements within the empire. Another one, however, came from the very core of the Ottoman elite created by these reforms. As the Empire increasingly adopted European law and principles and as its elite was increasingly in contact with European ideas, they also developed a sense of the Ottomans' unique heritage. A group of Ottoman intellectuals, the "Young Ottomans," started to formulate several criticisms toward the Tanzimat reforms. This group was formed around a nucleus of six figures who initially formed the "Patriotic Alliance" in 1876, and were both familiar with European ideas, along with the inner institutions of the Ottoman Empire.

The group grew to include hundreds of members, thus becoming extremely diverse in its ideology. They did formulate several ideas and criticisms toward the Sultan and the previous Tanzimat reforms. One of these was the perception that the Tanzimat had not tried to find compromise between the Islamic heritage and the European reforms and laws. The blind acceptance of European ideas and laws was criticized by members of the Young Ottomans, along with the lack of effort to overcome the differences between Islam and the West. Interestingly, this criticism did not come from conservative elements within the Ottoman society, but rather liberal and secular intellectuals. They were interested in the concept as a way to define a new form of Ottoman identity, which in retrospect was the main goal of the Young Ottomans. Islam played as much a role in this new identity, as did the more European concept of patriotism, or nationalism.

Another idea circulating among the Young Ottomans, the one that initially led to arrests and exiles among its members, was that the authority and power of the Sultan should be limited. One of the Young Ottomans' most prominent figures, Namik Kemal (1840-1888), derived from early Islamic traditions and practices the idea of a representative assembly that would balance the power of the Sultan. Both the idea that the Sultan's power needed to be checked along with their support for the enshrinement of Islamic tradition as the core of the Ottoman tradition led the Young Ottomans to see the necessity for the drafting of a Constitution. This Constitution would be the cornerstone of the new Ottoman identity, along with the Ottoman state and institutions.

Kemal

In 1876, following the deposition of Sultan Abdulaziz in a de facto coup fomented by the army and his ministers, Sultan Murad V came to power. His rule prompted a wave of optimism among the Young Ottomans, as the nephew of the former Sultan was known to be more liberal, and was largely brought to power by the former Grand Vizier Midhad Pasha, who was a supporter of the constitution. Yet Sultan Murad's rule was extremely short; he was deposed three months after taking power for suffering from a mental illness doctors found incurable. Midhad Pasha, who supported the ideas of the Young Ottomans, became Grand Vizier under Sultan Abdul Hamid II. Midhad Pasha's nomination enabled the drafting of the Ottoman Empire's first constitution, under the name "The Fundamental Law of the Sultanate."

Sultan Murad V

Sultan Abdul Hamid II

Yet, Sultan Abdul Hamid II and Midhad Pasha increasingly disagreed on the content of the constitution, particularly regarding the centralization of the Empire as well as the participation of minorities in the future institutions of the Empire. Sultan Abdul Hamid II had a much more centralized vision of the empire than Midhad Pasha, and did not see the participation of minorities as a priority. Midhad Pasha, on the other hand, sought for every people to participate in the future Parliament, to further consolidate the secular nature of the regime and convince European nations in helping the Ottoman Empire with its troubles in the Balkans. By guaranteeing a place to all the nations of the Empire, Midhad Pasha hoped to avoid a conflict with Russia, who increasingly used the Slavic populations as a pretext to act aggressively against the Ottomans. Sultan Abdul Hamid, and even some prominent Young Ottomans such as Namik Kemal opposed it. The idea was further seen by many among the Muslim population and elite as a pro-European Trojan horse that would see the influence of Christians rise further. Using that opposition, both coming from traditional segments of the elite and population, Sultan Abdul Hamid passed the Constitution on his terms, in a way that didn't threaten his privileges, and later sacked Midhad Pasha.

As fate would have it, the Constitutional era did not last long. Once the constitution came into effect and led to the creation of two chambers, the Chamber of Deputies and the Senate, both houses saw it as their duty to dismiss the ministers within the government who were perceived as corrupt. Claiming the dismissal of ministers was his prerogative, Sultan Abdul Hamid II requested a new election, which didn't, however, result in the outcome the Sultan sought to achieve. As a result, in 1878, he dissolved the Parliaments, and suspended the constitution. While Sultan Abdul Hamid never called for new elections, he did not abolish the constitution, so as to keep up appearances, but in reality the power shifted from the newly created class of bureaucrats back to the Sultan.

To counter the European influence and growing secularization of the Empire, both of which are seen by Abdul Hamid as negative, the new Sultan used his position as Caliph. During the decade that preceded his rise to power, the idea of pan-Islamism, which called for unity among Muslims, was supported by several scholars and member of the Ottoman elite, as a way to consolidate the Empire. While it failed to garner sufficient support prior to the rise of Abdul Hamid, the disastrous defeat of 1878 against Russia helped bolster its influence. The war was directly linked to the Balkan crisis, and the conditions of the Empire's Christian population (see the Rise of Nationalism). This fueled and legitimized to a certain extent efforts by Midhad Pasha to give more autonomy to these populations, and further improve the condition of the Christian populations within the Empire.

On the other hand, the fact that the passing of the Constitution did not prevent Russian intervention in the Balkans completely undermined those supporting a more inclusive political system. More importantly, the defeat resulted in the Treaty of San Stefano, marking the definitive loss of Serbia, Romania and Montenegro and the creation of the Principality of Bulgaria, as a vassal state of the Ottoman Empire, all of which were Christian territories. The percentage of non-Muslim subjects of the Empire was thus at its lowest in centuries, encouraging a policy that clearly moved away from the Tanzimat's inclusiveness.

Finally, and while not directly linked to the Russo-Turkish war of 1877-1878, the growing number of Muslim citizens of the French and British Empire meant the use of the Sultan's position as the Caliph was also seen as a possible bargaining tool in the relations between the two foreign powers and the Ottomans. Pan-Islamism was seen as a way to counter Europe's colonialism, and presented the heart of Islam as outside of Europe's reach. The development of other similar ideologies by the Empire's rival, namely the Pan-Hellenism supported by the Greeks, and Pan-Slavism used by Russia to fight the Ottomans, also served to increase the influence of Pan-Islamism among the ruling Ottoman Elite.

The rule of Sultan Abdul Hamid marked the end of the Tanzimat era. The Sultan saw the Tanzimat as a product of Europe's influence and strived to reverse it. Abdul Hamid used his position as the Caliph to try and federate the Muslim populations under the Ottoman rule. It should, however, be noted that the idea that the Ottoman Sultan is the Caliph of all Muslims was not obvious to every Muslim, given that he was neither an Arab, nor was a member of Muhammad's tribe.

Regardless, the rule of Abdul Hamid was marked by growing centralization as well as a focus on the Empire's Islamic and even Arab identity. This was not to say that Abdul Hamid's rule was one of total reversal of the progresses made during the Tanzimat. Under his rule, the Ottoman Empire continued to expand and modernize its administration and army. Major railways were built, including the Hejaz line from Damascus to Medina, the Baghdad railway and the Anatolia Railway. He also largely expanded the network of primary and secondary schools and created professional ones.

His influence was, however, largely limited by the scope of the crisis the Ottomans were experiencing. The Ottomans' default on the sovereign debt in 1875 just before the beginning of his reign forced him to accept the creation of the Ottoman Public Debt Administration (OPDA) in 1881, a European-controlled entity that employed between 5,000-9,000 employees in charge of collecting payments from various sources, meant to reimburse the debt. This included revenues from the salt, silk tithe, indirect taxes as well as various other agricultural products via several publicly-held companies.

While the OPDA did in fact both enable the modernization of the Ottoman agriculture and helped reduce the empire's debt, it also placed the focus on these products, rather than the industrialization of the country. It also largely limited the state's ability to interfere with these sectors. The relatively unfair trade due to the Capitulations treaty negotiated with several European powers, which included limitation on tariffs, as well as a growing worldwide competition on basic commodities due to the intensification of trade, all weighed on the Ottoman economy. The growth of nationalism, which had already been a major issue for the Ottoman Empire, also increasingly drew resources away from the modernization effort.

The Greek Revolution

Throughout the 19th century and the beginning of the 20th century, the rise of nationalistic aspirations largely contributed to the decline of the Ottoman Empire. The concept of "nation" was new to the Ottoman Empire, which had thus far thought of his subjects as communities built on religion rather than language or geographic origins. To deal with the challenges resulting from the existence of several religions within the Empire, the system of millet was created after Sultan Mehmed II conquered Constantinople. This system guaranteed that Christians, and later other religions, would be able to live under Ottoman law by allowing them to choose their own religious leaders, collect their taxes, use their own language and have their own court. While equality between the different subjects of the empire was not achieved (nor was it an actual goal until the Tanzimat era), the system made it possible for communities to live side by side. This system also preserved or created singularities among the various peoples of the Empire. In a sense, while the Millet system did indeed help the Empire's expansion and social stability for a time, it also prevented the tackling the issue of its identity, until it was too late, while also preserving, strengthening and helping to create new identities.

One of the strongest identities maintained through the Orthodox Church was a powerful elite group known as the *Phanariotes*, a Greek one. The existing Greek nationalistic sentiment had already been stirred by Russia, which saw the Greeks as allies in the struggle against the Ottomans. The new Russian intelligentsia saw the emerging Empire as the successor of the Byzantine Empire. This heritage was underlined by Russia's coat of arms, the double-headed eagle, formerly associated with Constantinople and the Eastern Roman Empire. On the political level, this narrative was seen as a way to influence the various peoples under Ottoman rule in the Balkans by attracting those who sought independence. It was no coincidence that Alexander Ypsilantis, a central figure of the Greek independence movement, served in the Russian army. However, the context of the uprising that broke out in 1821 made it different from previous revolts sponsored by Russia.

Ypsilantis

The aspirations of the peoples ruled by the Ottomans were fueled by the ideas of the French revolution in 1789. The revolution saw the emergence of the concept of "patrie" (Fatherland) and pitted the "patriotes" against the old nobility. The Greeks were particularly influenced by new ideas coming from Western Europe. Greek merchants travelled through Europe while elements among the Greek elite, the Phanariotes, cultivated their difference and supported the diffusion of such ideas by financing schools and books promoting it. This growth of the Greek national culture and sentiment, known as the Modern Greek Enlightenment, resulted in the sentiment among Greeks that they were part of one separate nation. In 1814, in the Russian city of Odessa,[5] these ideas led to the creation of a new secret society, the *Filiki Eteria* or Society of Friends, aimed at ending the Ottoman rule over Greece. The society attracted many members of the Greek diaspora. This included Ypsilantis, who became the head of the society on July 15, 1820, after the then Russian Foreign Minister and Ionian-born Ioannis Antonios Kapodistrias refused it.

Ypsilantis and the leaders of the *Filiki Eteria* designed a plan to obtain Greece's independence. At this time, while the Greek national sentiment was growing, the borders of the new country were uncertain, with some members of the society even backing the revival of the Byzantine Empire. Ypsilantis himself saw his fight as a broader struggle that should involve all the Christian subjects of the Empire, both for ideological and strategic purposes. He, along with other members of the secret society, felt that previous revolts in the region failed due to the lack of coordination between the organizers of the revolts. He thus drafted a plan that would involve simultaneous revolts led by Greeks, Serbs, Montenegrins, as well the subjects of Wallachia (present day Romania), Bulgaria and Moldavia.

In February 1821, with a small force of troops, Ypsilantis crossed the Prut River into Ottoman-held Moldavia, defeating the Turks and calling for a revolt in the Peloponnese and among Christian subjects of the Empire. Claiming he had secured the support of Russia, Ypsilantis was backed by Tudor Vladimirescu, the leader of the Wallachian Pandur militia, who occupied Bucharest on March 21. In Greece, Theodoros Kolokotronis, a member of the *Filiki Eteria*, captured the city of Tripolitsa in the Peloponnese, spreading the revolt to central Greece, Crete and Macedonia. Within a year, the revolutionaries took control of the Peloponnese and later repelled several Ottoman invasions.

Despite this success, the revolution was threatened both from within and from without. Ypsilantis's revolt in the Danube region had turned into a crushing defeat as Russia disavowed his campaign. The Tsar was then part of the Holy Alliance signed after the defeat of Napoleon that sought to preserve the status quo in Europe and prevent the circulation of revolutionary ideas. As a result, Vladimirescu withdrew his support for Ypsilantis as Ottoman troops crossed the Danube River and forced his retreat. In Greece, rivalries and dissensions between several

---

[5] Present day Ukraine.

factions within the liberated territories as well as between inhabitants of the Peloponnese and of central Greece hindered the war effort, eventually leading to a civil war.

The Greeks also faced an initially limited Egyptian intervention in Crete and Cyprus. The success of the Egyptian contingent eventually convinced the Ottomans to call for a broader intervention by Muhammad Ali Pasha, the Wali of Egypt, despite their defiance for the ambitious governor. During the years that followed, spearheaded by Egyptian troops, the Ottomans almost fully reconquered Greece, taking Athens in 1826.

Ultimately, the revolution was only saved by the intervention of European powers. While initially the *Holy Alliance* and its principles had prevented any intervention from European powers, public opinion shifted in favor of the insurgents quickly. The hanging of the Orthodox Patriarch Gregory V on suspicion of colluding with the rebels shocked the Europeans, and the support of inspiring figures such as Lord Byron, who fought alongside the rebels, helped grow the revolutionaries' support among the European nations. Britain, France and Russia signed the Treaty of London in 1827, calling for a cessation of hostilities, and stipulating that in case the Sultan would refuse, the powers could act to enforce such a cessation of hostilities. After the Sultan refused, Britain, France and Russia sent their fleets to the Peloponnese to pressure the Sultan. While it was initially only meant to prevent the Ottoman fleet from reaching the island of Hydra, an initial incident between a British boat and an Egyptian one triggered broader confrontations, resulting in the destruction of the Ottoman fleet during the Battle of Navarino. France later sent an expeditionary corps and, alongside the reorganized Greek forces, defeated the Ottomans at the Battle of Petra, in central Greece, leading eventually to the full independence of Greece in 1832.

A depiction of the patriarch shortly before his execution

Lord Byron

The revolution wasn't the first successful revolt against the Ottomans, but it was certainly a game-changer. For the first time, the Ottoman Empire was forced to recognize the full independence of a nation, not because of a war with a foreign power or an ambitious governor, but because of the aspirations of its people. The Filiki Eteria's attempt to prompt a larger uprising among Christians in the Balkans, despite being thwarted by the prompt Ottoman offensive, also left its mark in the memories of the Empire's subjects.

Moreover, the growing mistrust between the Empire and its subjects continued to be used by foreign powers such as Russia to weaken the Empire. The cause of the Ottoman Christians continued to be extremely popular among Europeans. As further shown by the initial intervention of the European powers, however, the goal was almost never to directly confront the Ottoman Empire, at least for England and France.

European Power Struggles

During the 19th century, the rivalry between France, England, and Russia was at the heart of what came to be known as the "Eastern Question." France and England were natural rivals, as both European powers were trying to build their colonial Empire. Despite that, their interests on several occasions aligned, particularly when it came to containing the growing expansion of the Russian Empire, which was increasingly seen as a threat and was building its own colonial Empire.

After the British victory against Napoleon, Britain was indisputably the leading global power. The British Empire expanded significantly toward Asia, driven by the advances of the East India Company, as well as the development of the steamship and telegraph. Britain acquired Singapore in 1819, Malacca in 1824, and expanded the profitable opium business to China. This expansion made it important for the British to expand their influence over the Ottoman territory, in light of its geographic position between Europe and Asia.

Napoleon's invasion of Egypt and later Syria, which forced a British intervention and was meant to hinder access to India and the East Indies, served to remind Britain of the Ottoman's strategic position – and its weakness. The British Empire's expansion and the British dominance made it a conservative power. England acted to maintain the "Pax Britannica" in British colonies, and global stability in British areas of influence. Under the leadership of Conservative leaders such as Benjamin Disraeli and Lord Salisbury, the British Empire adopted a foreign policy known as the "Splendid Isolation." This policy sought to maintain the global balance of power while limiting the need for any sort of British intervention in other powers' internal affairs along with any alliance that would demand a British intervention. This policy, which is one of nuance and, often times, ambiguity, stemmed from the global stature of the British Empire. England indeed quickly found out that, because of its expansion, a foreign power could be both its de facto ally on one issue, and its deadly enemy on others. This necessary ambiguity was at the heart of a long-lasting British reputation of unreliability and betrayal still present nowadays.

France's attitude towards the Ottoman Empire stemmed from the contradiction between the understanding that the Ottoman Empire was a necessary bulwark against the advances of Russia, France's colonialist aspiration, and growing sympathies for the emerging nationalistic movements. The first perception slowly disappeared as the Ottoman Empire weakened, while the second and third factors merged into a colonialist policy that pretended to emancipate perceived "inferior races" by colonizing them.

France's foreign policy in the 19th century was one of expansion and revenge. The idea that the French needed to seek revenge, initially against England and later against Prussia/Germany, was at the heart of France's colonialism. France lost almost all of its colonies in the wake of the Seven Years' War (1756-1763). The Napoleonic wars also served to show the limits of France's continental strategy, and the importance of building a potent navy to counter England. With Napoleon III in power, Prosper de Chasseloup-Laubat, the French Minister of the Navy and Colonies, strove to modernize the French Navy and be a central advocate of French colonial imperialism. Napoleon III's defeat further encouraged the development of colonies as France sought to counter-balance the traumatic loss of Alsace-Lorraine by expanding its Empire overseas. This policy, viewed positively by German Chancellor Otto von Bismarck as a way to shift the focus outside of Europe, was backed by Jules Ferry. Ferry supported what he called "the duty to civilize inferior races." This led to a French expansion both in North Africa with the establishment of a protectorate in Tunis (1881); Africa, with the occupation of Madagascar and the expansion of France's possession in Congo and Niger, and more importantly the development of the French "Indochine" in present-day Vietnam, Laos and Cambodia.

Prosper de Chasseloup-Laubat

In contrast with France and England's ambiguous attitude toward the Ottoman Empire,

Russia's stance was clear: the Ottoman Empire was an obstacle. This was driven by two elements, one geopolitical and the other political/cultural. The first was one that still explains the Russian foreign policy until today: access to the sea. This was a Russian obsession ever since the rule of Peter the Great (1672-1725), who fought against Sweden to gain access to the Baltic Sea as well as against the Ottoman Empire to gain access to the Black Sea. He was the founder of the Russian navy and one of the most significant Russian rulers, establishing Russia as a significant European power. The continuation of Peter the Great's race toward the sea has been a constant in Russian history. Regarding the Black Sea, Russia's ambition was to gain access to the Mediterranean, which was controlled by Constantinople.

This geopolitical interest was also fueled by several political and cultural movements. This included the pan-slavism ideology, which sought to unite all of the Slavic people, as well as the "Megali Idea" (Great Idea), which sought to revive the Byzantine Empire. Influential figures, including Fyodor Dostoyevsky, as well as part of the Orthodox Church, supported the idea that Muslim Ottomans should be replaced by a reinvigorated Byzantine Empire, a natural ally of which would be Russia, the "Third Rome." Russia's growing influence in the Caucasus also enabled the launching of two-pronged offensives, both from the north of the Ottoman Empire and the east. This proved fatal to the Empire during World War I

The Russian intervention in the Greek independence war and the battle of Navarino prompted the closure of the Dardanelles strait. As always, when its access to the sea was threatened, Russia reacted swiftly. In April-June of 1828, a Russian force of more than 90,000 soldiers, led by Tsar Nicholas I, invaded Wallachia and Moldavia. The main Russian force crossed the Danube and entered the Dobruja region, laying siege to three Ottoman fortresses. When the siege of Shumla, one of the three Ottoman citadels, proved initially difficult, the Tsar sent a new army, defeating the Ottomans during the Battle of Kulevicha on June 11, 1829.

Tsar Nicholas I

Russia also successfully opened a second front in the Caucasus, initially aimed at drawing Turkish forces away from the European front. This strategy proved more than effective with the capture of Kars, Akhaltsikhe, and Erzurum in Eastern Turkey. As a result, the treaty of Adrianople in 1829 marked the Ottoman defeat and the loss of part of the remaining Black Sea coast, parts of modern-day Armenia, as well as the occupation of Moldavia and Wallachia by Russia, until the Crimean War.

The Crimean War was particularly interesting due to its initial trigger, the giant political standoff that preceded it, the geopolitical changes at work, and their result on the balance of power at the time. On a broader geopolitical scope, the fact that France and Britain sided with the Ottomans against Russia highlighted concerns over the growing threat represented by Russian ambition in the Black Sea. Russia's reaction to the crisis was also a sign of the importance of this area, a key to Moscow's ability to project its power outside of its natural area of influence. The recent war in Ukraine, and Russian intervention in Syria which began by the sending of ships from Sebastopol to Tartus may also be a good reminder of the strategic value of this region.

The actual trigger to the crisis – though the war had much deeper roots - was also significant, underscoring growing rivalries over the holy sites in Jerusalem and Bethlehem and the emergence of religious tensions there. Tensions between France and Russia indeed increased years before the war after a series of incidents surrounding the Christian holy sites in Palestine. Local disputes between the Roman Christians and Orthodox worshipers often broke out in front of the Church of the Holy Sepulchre – the Ottomans even had to place soldiers in front of the site during the holidays. In 1846, a dispute after the Easter mass resulted in clashes that killed as many as 40 worshipers. These tensions, along with the growing number of Russian visitors, resulted in growing anger and concerns amongst the French Christians, who argued that France had been the protector of the holy sites ever since the Crusades, a right that was confirmed by the Capitulations treaty of 1740. The Russians, however, maintained that they had been the protectors of all Christians within the Empire since the signing of the Kuchuk Kainarji treaty in 1774.

A picture of the Church of the Holy Sepulchre from
http://www.flickr.com/photos/jlascar/

France's president, Louis-Napoleon, the soon-to-be Napoleon III, saw an opportunity to garner support from the "clerical party," the Christian conservative movement ahead of his planned coup. The French Ambassador to the "Sublime Porte"[6] and a member of the clerical party, Marquis Charles de La Valette, threatened the Ottomans – and thus indirectly the Russians.

---

[6] A metonym for the Ottoman central government, referring to the old tradition of announcing the Sultan's decisions at the gate (porte) of his Palace in Constantinople.

According to La Valette, France was ready to take "extreme measures" to enforce France's "historical" role as the protectors of Christians within the Empire. The threat in turn led to a diplomatic escalation during which Russia threatened to suspend all diplomatic relations with the Ottoman Empire should it accept France's demand.

Napoleon III

In November 1852, Louis-Napoleon sent a French ship, the *Charlemagne*, to Constantinople to pressure the Sultan into giving France control over the administration of the holy sites. This was a bold move. The deployment of the 80-gun ship of the line to Constantinople violated the 1841 London Strait treaty, according to which both the Dardanelles and Bosphorus Straits between the Black Sea and the Mediterranean were to be sealed to all warships. Napoleon's move may have been perceived at the time as just another escalation to an ongoing crisis, but it wasn't. The purpose of the deployment of the *Charlemagne* was in fact part of a broader French effort to sabotage the pillars of European stability that were established after the defeat of Louis-

Napoleon's uncle, Napoleon Bonaparte. France was frustrated with the current status quo, which favored England. By blatantly violating the treaty, France threatened an agreement that largely protected the British influence in the Mediterranean from Russian expansionism, and forced Russia to show its true intentions. The Russians were not truly interested in the fate of the holy sites, and France wasn't either; the fate of the Ottoman Empire was what was truly in the balance, and the Russian ambition to control the straits clearly threatened the status quo that Britain had tirelessly tried to protect.

Russia initially retaliated by mobilizing 100,000 soldiers in Bessarabia, near the northern border of the Ottoman Empire. In February 1853, France seemed to back off as Napoleon III replaced his "hawkish" Ambassador, Charles de La Valette. The newly crowned Emperor[7] indeed seemed to have lost interest in the cause of the Christians after he asserted his power and overthrew the Second Republic. However, the move may also have been meant to prompt an even stronger Russian response and make sure British efforts to find a diplomatic solution to the crisis would fail.

Regardless, British efforts indeed failed. Russia sent a delegation to Constantinople led by General Alexander Menshikov, who made unacceptable demands that offended the Ottomans, French, and British. Menshikov, for the sake of protecting Orthodox Christians, demanded the right to intervene in any part of the Empire that included such populations, as well as making Russia an official protectorate over the millions of Christian Orthodox subjects of the Ottoman Empire. This was equivalent to the de facto annexation by Russia of the remaining Ottoman provinces in Europe, and it would certainly have meant the fall of the Ottoman Empire by turning it into a Russian vassal. These demands showed that Russia sought to settle once and for all the "Eastern Question," at least in Europe, betting that England and Austria would support the move in a bid to establish their own area of influence.

---

[7] Louis Napoleon was crowned on December 2, 1852, a year after the coup that ended the Second Republic. The crowning and coup is also a clear attempt to place himself as Napoleon I's successor, as December 2 is also the anniversary of the Battle of Austerlitz.

Menshikov

On October 5, 1853, the Ottoman Empire declared war on Russia. While the decision was prompted by the recognition that the Ottoman Empire was in mortal danger, this was still a leap of faith. The British and French deployed their fleet in the Aegean Sea, yet Russia was in contact with the British government and sought to secure England's support, or at least its neutrality.

The decision to declare war was issued without any solid promise being made by either France or England regarding an intervention to support the Turks. The Ottomans, however, showed their understanding of the local "great game" and recognized that it was in London's and Paris's interest to intervene should the war not go in their favor. Despite an initial success at the Battle of Oltenitza in December, the Ottomans, faced with the prospect of several Russian-backed revolts in the Balkans, decided to shift their military focus on the Caucasus. As they did so, the Russians, who understood that the upcoming offensive relied on the sending of reinforcements through the Black Sea, attacked and destroyed the Ottoman naval forces during the Battle of Sinop. The Ottomans were also defeated twice on the ground in the Caucasus.

Napoleon III exploited this in a bid to convince England that an intervention was necessary by threatening to act unilaterally should London fail to protect the Ottoman Empire. On January 3,

1854, both the French and British Navy crossed the Bosphorus strait to the Black Sea. The allies agreed on a broader intervention in Crimea, meant to alleviate the military pressure on the Ottoman Empire and hinder Russian naval expansionism. French and British forces landed north of the Russian stronghold of Sebastopol, the home of the Black Sea fleet.

After several ground battles, the allies started the particularly long siege of the city of Sebastopol itself. What was meant to be a triumphal march toward the city turned into a protracted siege despite the heavy naval bombardment. French and British forces attempted to secure strategic positions for their artillery while later pushing eastward toward the city of Azov to draw Russian troops away from Sebastopol and cut the Russian supply lines.

The siege was finally successful in September 1855, after a series of deadly battles and a renewed bombardment of the city that involved hundreds of cannons. Celebrations were held in Paris and London because the fall of Sebastopol was seen as the end of a war that had grown increasingly unpopular, but the Tsar, who saw an opportunity to counter-balance the allies' military success, threatened a renewed campaign in the Balkans. The Tsar gave the impression that he was prepared for a protracted conflict that would draw French and British troops inside Russia. Russia knew how to play on French fears regarding a new, disastrous "Russian campaign"[8] and both sides sued for peace, achieving it with the Treaty of Paris.

While very few territorial changes were made, the conflict led to the demilitarization of the Black Sea, marking the decline of Russian influence there. It certainly extended the life of the "sick man of Europe." On a broader level, the Crimean War marked the end of the Holy Alliance and the status quo in Europe, leading to a broader reorganization in Europe, and the beginning of a series of conflicts between European powers which would eventually be fatal to the Sublime Porte.

During the late 1850s and the early 1860s, the precarious European balance of power crumbled. The war between Austria and France in Italy, and the rise of a new central power during the war of unification led by Otto Von Bismarck, destroyed the status quo. Napoleon III's final defeat, as well as the alliance with the rising Prussian power, gave Russia enough room to brush aside the treaties signed in the wake of the Crimean War and revived its past ambitions fueled by a desire for revenge. Several revolts in the Balkans provided the perfect pretext. In 1875, a Serbian revolt broke out in Herzegovina, and spread to Bosnia. Local officials and Bosnian landowners resisted the reforms implemented during the Tanzimat, angering the Christian populations who suffered from the burden of rising taxes. As it was on the verge of bankruptcy, the Ottoman government also raised taxes across the Empire.

Ensuring the support of nearby Christian communities, local rebels fomented a revolt that rapidly spread to other Ottoman provinces. The revolt spread to nearby Bulgaria in April 1876.

---

[8] In reference to the French invasion of Russia during the Napoleonic wars.

In response, the Ottoman Empire mobilized irregulars, the "bashi-bazouks," to quell the rebellion. These were made up of local Muslims, as well as refugees from previous wars, including Circassians who fled the Russian advances. The revolt was brutally put down, drawing significant criticism from European powers. Bashi-bazouks, known for their lack of discipline, massacred the local population of several villages. In Europe, the Turks got a reputation for their cruelty and violence while Abdul Hamid II got a new nickname: the "Red Sultan."

On April 24, 1877, Russia declared war on the Ottoman Empire, less than a year after Serbia and Montenegro had done so. Russian forces marched through Romania, which declared its independence on May 10, 1877, and defeated the Ottomans in Bulgaria. They then headed toward Thrace and took the city of Adrianople, just west of Constantinople, in January 1878.

Though it would survive for nearly another half century, the Ottoman Empire was fatally wounded in this war. This time, the war brought about what the previous confrontations with Russia would have become if the European powers had not intervened. Russian troops were marching toward Constantinople, and as they became alarmed by this swift Russian victory and its potential consequences, the British forced Russia to accept a truce on January 31. The unfolding negotiations would lead to the formal recognition of the independence of Romania, Serbia and Montenegro, as well as the autonomy of Bulgaria, Bosnia and Herzegovina. With that, the Ottoman Empire had lost almost all of its European provinces, and it would most likely have lost all of them if it weren't for a second European intervention that forced Russia to modify the initial Treaty of San Stefano, which would have included the loss of Macedonia and Eastern Rumelia to the newly independent Bulgaria.

The Ottoman Empire was clearly declining, and humiliated. In the wake of the defeat, the Sublime Porte lost Tunisia in 1881, as it became a French protectorate, and an already autonomous Egypt, which fell under the British administration in 1882.

A Brutal End

The Young Turks emerged in the wake of the Abdul Hamid's suspension of the constitution in 1878, largely from the ranks of the new bureaucratic and intellectual elite created by the Tanzimat period. They were a diverse conglomerate of underground opposition movements, the most prominent of which was the Committee for Union and Progress (CUP), who sought to preserve the Ottoman Empire through reforms and oppose the autocratic rule of the Sultan.

The Young Turks' movement started with the founding of a new secret society on July 14, 1889, the 100 anniversary of Bastille Day, in the Military Medicine University of Istanbul. It largely recruited its first members from among similar military academies across the country, the Empire's high-ranking civil servants, and the Turkish diaspora, particularly in France (where Ahmed Riza became a prominent figure and later the head of the CUP).

Riza

While it became increasingly popular amongst the young generation of the Ottoman elite, the movement was diverse, including both various ethnical groups as well as opposing ideologies and programs. Three main ideologies would divide the Young Turks' movement. The first, a pro-Western movement that sought to implement radical secular reforms, viewed Islam as an obstacle.

The second came from admirers of the Japanese "Meiji era" and Japan's ability to adopt Western technology and reforms while keeping its unique identity. This movement, the influence of which would be bolstered by Japan's victory over Russia in 1905, sought to preserve Islam as the core of the Empire while deepening the reforms implemented during the Tanzimat.

The third one was a nationalistic movement seeking to preserve the Ottoman Empire by centralizing the state, and putting an emphasis on the "Turkishness" of the Empire. This growing idea showed that the nationalistic wave that started at the beginning of the eighteenth century finally reached the heart of the Empire.

Despite their diversity and contradictions, the Young Turks all agreed that the Constitution was the most solid basis for reforms and criticized Abdul Hamid's authoritarian rule, as well as his perceived dependence on European powers.

For his part, Abdul Hamid understood that the party's diverse ideology was both its strength and its weakness. Seeking to show the limits of the Young Turks' idealism and break their unity, he appointed several Young Turks to his administration, thus briefly delegitimizing the movement. Nonetheless, the movement continued to expand even within the Sultan's entourage, with members including Damad Mahmud Pasha, Abdul Hamid's brother in law, and his two sons.

The movement also particularly attracted officers of the Ottomans' Third Army, stationed in the province of Macedonia,[9] where the decline of the Ottoman Empire was particularly visible. Macedonia was experiencing a state of lawlessness and rampant civil war stemming from the activity of rival nationalistic factions, often sponsored by local states, who fought the Ottomans when they were not busy fighting each other. The absence of authority helped the expansion of the Young Turks' movement, both by showing the need for reforms, and by giving unprecedented authority to the officers in charge of quelling the multiple insurgencies. A widespread problem of clientelist promotions and corruptions that plagued the army at the time also justified the idea of revolution among frustrated officers within the army who saw inept commanders rise through the ranks of the military because of their connections rather than their abilities. As a result, Salonika, a major center for the various currents within the Young Turks, became an intellectual hub where new ideas that would change the Middle East grew. It is no coincidence that Mustafa Kemal, the future Ataturk, grew up in Salonika, nor was it a coincidence that a little-known man named David Grun, who became Israel's first Prime Minister under the name David Ben Gurion, studied in the city.

In June 1908, a meeting between the King of England, Edward VII, and Russian Tsar Nicholas II in the city of Reval[10] raised an alarm among the Young Turks' officers within the Third Army. The meeting was meant to end several disputes between Russia and the British, particularly regarding Persia and Central Asia, and it led to the Anglo-Russian Entente in August. On the side of this meeting, however, several statements were made pointing at a possible partition of Macedonia. During the same month, the Sultan opened an investigation into the presence of CUP cells within the Third Army; uncovering a CUP cell within the army. Major Ismail Enver, a member of the Young Turks stationed in Salonika, refused to leave for Constantinople, where he had been recalled for a promotion. Fearing that the alleged promotion was a trap, he fled alone into the mountains.

---

[9] At the time, the Ottoman province of Macedonia included parts of modern-day Greece, Macedonia, Bulgaria, Serbia and Albania.
[10] Present day Tallinn, the capital of Estonia

Enver

Understanding the danger they were facing, several officers led by Major Ahmed Niyazi within the Third Army organized a revolt. Following Enver's example, Niyazi decamped and took refuge in the mountains with 200 men. The revolt rapidly spread to other parts of the Province. Abdul Hamid's attempts to quell the revolt all failed, with military units either refusing to go to Macedonia or fraternizing with the insurgents. On July 23, Sultan Abdul Hamid was forced to revive the 1876 Constitution, paving the way for general elections largely won by the CUP and the Liberal Union (LU), a rival Young Turk party supporting decentralization.

The revolution initially prompted a wave of celebrations across the Empire, as the more liberal ideology among the Young Turks seemed to triumph. In a speech given in the aftermath of the Young Turks' success, Enver stated, "Henceforth, we are all brothers. There are no longer

Bulgars, Greeks, Roumans, Jews, Mohammedans; under the same blue sky we are all equal and proud Ottomans."

In reality, the Young Turks' movement was divided, and the revolution accelerated the partition of the Empire. The revolution and subsequent fall of the Sultan's authoritarian rule was seen as an opportunity by various nations and empires to further their cause and interests. Celebrations were short-lived. In October, Bulgaria proclaimed its formal independence with the support of the Russian Tsar. A day after, the Austro-Hungarian Empire, concerned about the possibility that the revolution would spread to Bosnia-Herzegovina and lead to its independence, annexed the region. In Crete, a newly formed Parliament announced its union with Greece. The revolution also prompted the creation of the Young Arab Society (al-Fatat), which sought to defend the rights of the Arabs within the Empire and demanded Arab soldiers serve only in Arab provinces.

Within the Ottoman Empire itself, a rumbling Islamic counter-revolution prompted a broad crackdown on Islamic figures. The Young Turks rightfully accused the Sultan, who maintained symbolic power, of fueling dissent and opposition to their reforms. Indeed, in April 1909, theological students, clerics and several military units revolted after the Sultan promised he would restore the Caliphate and get rid of secular policies. Troops loyal to the Young Turks from the Third Army entered Istanbul and quelled the rebellion on April 24. Among them were the already notorious Ismail Enver, as well as the promising Mustafa Kemal. Three days later, Abdul Hamid II was deposed, exiled, and replaced by his brother, Mehmed V.

Mehmed V

In October 1911, Italian soldiers, along with troops from the Italian Somaliland and Eritrea, landed in Tripolitania in present day Libya. Italy's claim over the last Ottoman province in North Africa stemmed from verbal agreements with France and England. The two leading powers of the time offered to balance the French protectorate over Tunisia and British control over Cyprus by creating an Italian colony in Libya. This agreement was not enforced until 1911, when Italy felt threatened by the growing French expansionism in North Africa, which could see the western Mediterranean becoming a "French Lake." Libya was also seen as a door to sub-Saharan Africa and a potential commercial hub.

The invasion itself was short. While the Ottoman army managed to launch a successful counter-offensive led by Mustafa Kemal against Italian troops in Tobruk, it was rapidly overwhelmed when Italy sent further reinforcements. The modernization of the Ottoman army wasn't complete at the time, particularly within the Ottoman Navy, which still relied mostly on wooden ships. The Italian military employed modern military equipment and would carry out the first airstrikes in military history during the campaign. In October 1912, the Ottoman army was defeated, and a treaty was signed asserting Italian control over Libya, despite the fact that the invasion triggered a significant Arab rebellion against the Ottomans.

The swift defeat of the Ottoman military convinced the Balkan nations that the empire was finished, and Greece, Bulgaria, Serbia and Montenegro had been waiting for a chance to seize the remaining Ottoman possessions in Europe. The weakening of the Ottoman influence in its last European stronghold was further illustrated by the Albanian revolts of 1910 and 1912, which saw a Muslim population turn against the Young Turks. While the Ottoman army was still deployed in Libya, in October 1912 they all declared war on the Ottoman Empire. The Ottoman army, weakened by the war with Italy, was defeated by the coalition of Balkan nations. Salonika, the heart of the Young Turks' revolution, was occupied, along with Edirne, just west of Istanbul.

While the Ottomans had a chance to recapture Edirne as the former allies started turning against each other, the war had changed the Young Turks. The idea that fraternity amongst the communities forming the Empire could eventually save it was brushed aside by nationalistic realities. In the provinces freed by the Balkan coalition, emerging nations were waging war against each other, leading to the displacement of thousands of Muslims. The borders created by the conflict were unstable. For instance, the heart of the Albanian revolt, Kosovo, was given to Serbia. As a result of the defeat, the Young Turks grew more nationalistic, putting an emphasis on the Turkish identity, and ethnic homogeneity. Beyond that, the feeling that the Ottoman Empire was being dismantled by their so-called allies, namely France and England, as well as changes within the Young Turks, sealed the Ottomans' alliance with Germany.

The Ottomans' relations with Germany were not new. In the same way that France sought the support of the Sublime Porte in its fight against central European powers during the 16th century, Germany saw the Ottoman Empire as a possible strategic partner against Russia, France, and England. German Kaiser Wilhelm II visited the Ottoman Empire on two occasions before World War I and sought to encourage Abdul Hamid's pan-Islamism, which he saw as a useful tool against the British colonialism. During his second visit in 1898, the Kaiser visited the tomb of Saladin in Damascus and offered to pay for its renovation. Arab newspapers praised the visit, stating that the Kaiser was "the best friend of the great Sultan;" and "the most sincere and loyal monarch in his friendship toward the Sultan." The German Emperor even earned the title of "Hajji Wilhelm."

Wilhelm II

Economic relations expanded with the building of the Baghdad Railway, starting in 1903. The Prussian and later German military expertise was also increasingly used by the Ottoman army, peaking with the German mission of 1913, led by German military officer Otto Liman von Sanders.

Despite that, the Ottoman Empire did not initially seek to formally ally with Germany, much less participate in a global conflict. In fact, as the 1910s dawned, the growing rivalry between the Entente alliance (France, Russia, and Britain)[11] and the Central Powers (the Austro-Hungarian Empire and Germany), seemed like a distant problem. Ironically, the Ottoman Empire sought on multiple occasions to enter into an alliance with the British, French and Russians, or to at least

---

[11] Referring to the Triple Entente, an agreement between these three powers signed in the wake of the "Entente Cordiale" (Cordial Friendship) treaty between France and England in 1904 and the Anglo-Russian Entente of 1907.

secure an agreement regarding its neutrality during a potential conflict. The alliance with Russia was, however, more central to the British and French, who refused the various Ottoman proposals.

The disastrous war against the Balkan states brought together the changes needed to convince the Ottomans of the benefit of the alliance with the Kaiser. As the war broke out, Enver Pasha[12] (Ismail Enver) returned from Libya to Istanbul on January 1913. Three days after his arrival, he participated in a coup against the Turkish government led by the CUP's rival, the LU. Together with Talaat Pasha and Djemal Pasha, they formed a dictatorial triumvirate dubbed the "Three Pashas." Enver played a critical role in the empire's entry into the coming war on the side of Germany; he had been the Empire's military attaché and was convinced that a military alliance with the Germany would be beneficial.

Enver's conviction stemmed from his perception of the Kaiser's military strength, as well as the understanding that while the Entente did not need the Ottomans to win the war, Germany did, and the Germans would thus act to strengthen the Ottomans. He also represented the military officers among the Young Turks who admired the Prussian state and the central role played by the army in the building of the German nation. Finally, his decision to back an alliance with Germany stemmed from the belief that the upcoming war between the European nations would be a short one that could present opportunities to counter-balance the Ottomans' territorial losses at the expense of Russia and England.

Nonetheless, he was the only one among the Three Pashas to believe in the German-Ottoman alliance. Both Djemal and Talaat Pasha favored an alliance with the Entente, while Sultan Mehmed V supported the empire's neutrality. The Ottomans' pledge for an alliance with the British failed in 1913, along with a later request made by Talaat Pasha to Russia and another one to France made by Djemal Pasha. Enver swayed Djemal Pasha, and on July 22, 1914, six days before the official beginning of World War I, the Ottomans officially offered the signing of an alliance with Germany.

Despite the initial reluctance of the German foreign office, which feared the Ottomans' weakness would be a burden, the Kaiser pushed for an alliance that he saw as a way to divert forces from other critical fronts. On August 2, the secret alliance between the Ottoman Empire and Germany, an alliance that would be fatal to the old empire, was signed. In the wake of the agreement, on October 29, the Ottoman fleet, reinforced by two German naval ships, carried out a surprise attack on the Russian Black Sea fleet, prompting a declaration of war by the Entente powers.

During World War I, the Ottoman Empire fought a multi-pronged war that would greatly strain its resources, leading to starvation and great suffering for the local populations. In the east, the

---

[12] Pasha is an honorary title given, originally, to military commanders.

Russians opened the war with an offensive in the Caucasus a few days after the Ottomans' surprise attack. This front would be one of the toughest in the war, not only because of the Russian human resources but also because of the climate and strategic mistakes by the Ottoman military leadership. Enver Pasha, the Ottoman Minister of War, was hoping that a swift victory against Russia would lay the groundwork for Turkey's expansion in the Caucasus and a revolt of local Muslim populations. In this, Enver was guided by his "Pan-Turkism," which sought to create a Turkish region in the Caucasus.

As the Russian offensive began, Enver ordered the launching of a complex attack against the Russian forces, disregarding the opinion of General Hasan Izzet Pasha, the commander of the Third Army based in eastern Turkey. In December, as the front stabilized despite the initial failed offensive, Enver sent one of his emissaries to Izzet Pasha, ordering a planned spring offensive on Sarikamis to be launched immediately. Enver believed that with superior numbers (the Ottomans had a force of more than 110,000 men while the Russians only had 65,000) the Turkish force would be able to swiftly encircle and destroy the Russian army. The Ottoman army, however, was ill-equipped, poorly trained and lacked the proper experience of mountain warfare to carry on such a complex operation.

Izzet

Faced with Izzet Pasha's reluctance to launch such a risky operation in a mountainous area during the winter, Enver left Istanbul to take personal command of the offensive. After a failed assault on Russian positions, the Ottoman army withdrew to regroup and launch a new attempt. During the march, the cold, mountainous terrain and exhaustion of the Ottoman troops resulted in devastating casualties. The 10th Corps, for instance, lost 90% of its soldiers in what came to be called the "Death March."

Enver's Sarikamis offensive ended in a disaster. Epidemics and a renewed Russian offensive deepened the blow the following year. This disaster was rapidly blamed on the Armenians, who had supposedly betrayed the Ottoman Empire. In April 1915, Armenian intellectuals in Istanbul were executed, paving the way for the first large-scale genocide in modern history. Russian advances would only be stopped by the Bolshevik Revolution in 1917, which took Russia out of the war entirely.

In Mesopotamia,[13] a British force mostly made of Indian soldiers from the British Empire launched an offensive in the south in November 1914, by first taking Basra. While the British initially only sought to protect their oil interests, including the nearby complex of Abadan, the swift capture of Basra convinced them of the benefits of a campaign in Mesopotamia. The British force was ordered to march towards Kut, north of Basra. Understanding the threat posed by the offensive, Enver Pasha sent reinforcements to Baghdad and ordered the launch of a counter-offensive to retake the Shatt al-Arab.[14] The local Ottoman commander, instead, waged a successful but costly defensive war, leading to the initial surrender of the British force under Major General Charles Townshend. The British, however, sent a new commander, General Stanley Maude, along with reinforcements and ordered the expansion of the port of Basra, leading to a new offensive against Kut. The offensive was successful, opening the way for the capture of Baghdad in 1916 and an offensive in the Anbar province in 1917-18.

---

[13] Present-day Iraq.
[14] The confluence of the Euphrates and Tigris.

Maude

Meanwhile, in the west, close to Istanbul, the Entente's inability to carry out a naval siege of the capital led to the sending of a French and British expeditionary force that landed on the mainland in April 1915. The Ottomans knew the Dardanelles strait would most certainly be attacked and had prepared significant defenses. The plan drafted by the then First Lord of the Admiralty, Winston Churchill, was meant to destroy Ottoman defenses along the Dardanelles. However, allied forces made of British, Irish, Australian and New Zealanders were unable to penetrate the Ottoman defenses, advancing only about 100 meters from the shores. The Ottomans, led by German General Liman von Sanders, further reinforced their positions. The later attempt of the British to establish a new beachhead was more successful, yet the British government refused to send significant reinforcements.

Churchill in the early 20th century

In December 1915, what was certainly the most successful part of the Gallipoli offensive, the evacuation of the British forces began. The Ottomans' successful defense of the Dardanelles led to Churchill's resignation. More importantly, it bolstered the rising popularity of Mustafa Kemal, then Lieutenant Colonel, and offered hope that the Ottomans could indeed counter-balance their territorial losses.

Earlier, in January 1915, the Ottomans had launched their first offensive in the Sinai. Djemal Pasha, one of the "Three Pashas," as the newly appointed governor of Greater Syria,[15] participated in the planning of an offensive that meant to threaten the Suez Canal and British

---

[15] Present-day Syria, Israel/Palestinian Territories, Lebanon and northern Iraq.

domination of Egypt. While the Ottoman forces reached the canal, with some units even crossing it, a strong British defense prevented them from advancing. British naval units deployed in the Great Bitter Lake bombed the only bridgehead created during the costly offensive. By February, the Ottoman force had pulled back to Gaza.

The successful defense of Gallipoli, however, convinced both Enver and Djemal that a second operation should be launched. Reinforcements arrived from Gallipoli and the Ottomans launched the second attempt in August 1916. British forces had, however, moved eastward toward Palestine, and they defeated the Ottoman forces at the Battle of Romani. The battle was the first clear British victory over the Ottomans and their German allies, resulting in a successful counter-offensive that led British General Edmund Allenby in Jerusalem. A final push with the Megiddo offensive and renewed campaign in Mesopotamia brought Entente forces even further into the Ottoman Empire.

The Arab revolt has been engraved in modern memories by movies such as *Lawrence of Arabia* as a widespread nationalistic movement against the cruel Ottoman occupier. The reality is far more complex. In 1914, as the Ottomans entered the war, the Arabs' loyalty to the Sultan and Caliph was not in question. Arab nationalism did indeed emerge in the wake of the revolution of 1908, but it mostly attracted Arab intellectuals as the local population remained loyal subjects of the Empire. European encroachment on several former Ottoman provinces such as Algeria, Libya, Tunisia and Egypt made the danger of a possible Arab revolt relatively clear.

The abundant, one-sided and relatively romanced view the West may have of the "Arab Revolt" also largely ignored the belief among the Ottomans and their allies that Muslims beyond the empire's borders would rise against their colonial masters. Before the famous British campaign led by Thomas Edward Lawrence to use Arab nationalism against the Ottomans, the Ottomans themselves attempted to use the Islamic faith against the British and French. In November 1914, this belief led the empire's head of Religious Affairs, Shaikh ul-Islam, to declare jihad against the Entente powers. In Germany, Max von Oppenheim, who was at the time considered one of the leading experts in the Middle East, successfully convinced the German Foreign Office that the Ottomans could stir up rebellions among Arab subjects of the colonial powers. He headed the newly created *Nachrichtenstelle für den Orient* (Intelligence Bureau for the East), dispatching agents to foment nationalistic movement both in the Arab world and in Asia. The Bureau also sent Wilhelm Wassmuss to Persia to fuel anti-British sentiment, while anti-French propaganda was distributed in Morocco, as were pan-Islamic documents in Egypt during the Ottoman offensive in the Sinai.

T.E. Lawrence

In Libya, German and Ottoman influence encouraged the Senussi revolt of Sayyid Ahmad al-Sharif. The Senussi had successfully prevented the consolidation of an Italian presence in the Fezzan region of southern Libya, and kept good relations with the Ottomans. Following Italy's entry into the war, the conflict between the Senussi and Italy became part of the global struggle. Ahmad al-Sharif had broad ambitions and was leading the war against the Italians under the title of *Amir al-Muminin* (the commander of the faithful) in Africa. Ahmad al-Sharif spearheaded an offensive from the Siwa Oasis in Egypt toward the coast, between November 1915 and February 1917. The offensive forced British forces to retreat to the coastal city of Matruh, before they regained the advantage in 1916-1917.

The danger posed by this particular attempt to both foment dissent in Egypt, launch an attack in Sinai, and encourage an offensive from Syria was not to be brushed aside, and it did raise significant concerns among the British. Maude's[16] risky decision to push his offensive towards Baghdad and stretch his supply line was at least partly explained by these concerns. In Cairo, Sir

---

[16] The British commander of the expeditionary force in Basra mentioned previously.

Henry McMahon, the British High Commissioner in Egypt, saw the danger behind the Ottomans' move. This menace was likely in McMahon's mind as he corresponded with Hussein Bin Ali, the Sharif of Mecca. The prospect of a revolt in the Arab peninsula seemed like a clever way to deflect Ottoman pressures on Egypt.

Sharif Hussein was not known to be an Arab nationalist, but the discovery of an alleged plot by the Young Turks to replace Hussein with a rival member of his family made him suspicious of the Ottoman's intentions. Hussein's nomination by Sultan Abdul Hamid may have prompted concerns that he would be removed by the CUP, and already led to unsuccessful contacts with the British before World War I. His son, Faisal, was sent to Istanbul to clarify the situation and returned convinced that the plot was real. On his way, he decided to accept the support of the Young Arab Society,[17] which he had met before in Damascus. The situation in Greater Syria also largely changed as Djemal Pasha, returning from his first failed Sinai offensive, received emergency power in the province. A plot was supposedly discovered in Beirut, confirming what Djemal Pasha suspected: The Arab intelligentsia was planning to betray the Empire. There were certainly some Arab intellectuals who sought independence, and the Young Arab Society had indeed already reached out to Sharif Hussein. However, the actual support they received was relatively limited; even Faisal was initially unconvinced, and only agreed to receive their support after traveling to Istanbul. Regardless, as a result, 11 Arab intellectuals from Beirut were hanged in August 1915. In the following months, Djemal Pasha earned the title of *al-Saffah*, the Blood Shedder.

---

[17] See chapter on the 1908 Revolution.

Sharif Hussein

As Faisal returned, Sharif Hussein continued to correspond with McMahon and was convinced by the British Commissioner that the Arabs would receive an independent Arab state in the wake of the Ottoman defeat. With the capture of Mecca in July 1916 after a month of urban fighting, Hussein began a successful offensive that would help achieve the final victory against the Ottoman Empire. The acts of sabotage, guerilla warfare and the capture of Aqaba proved that the British move was tactically right, as Allenby's forces broke through the Ottomans' defense, culminating with the capture of Damascus in 1918.

During this time, and despite McMahon's promises, the Asia Minor Agreement[18] between

---

[18] The official name of the Sykes-Picot agreement.

French diplomat Georges Picot and his British counterpart, Mark Sykes, divided the French and British influence in the Middle East. The deal was the result of broader discussions with Russia, which initially sought to divide the Ottoman Empire into three main area of influence: The northern parts (Turkey) would have been under Russian influence, and the southern parts (between Mesopotamia and Palestine) would be under British influence, while the French influence in Lebanon and Syria would represent a buffer zone between the two. The Bolshevik revolution in 1917, however, prevented the realization of these discussions, leading to the Sykes-Picot agreement.

The deal was partially leaked by the Russian newspapers *Izverstia* and *Pravda*, as well as by the *Guardian* through a Russian source. While the exact borders of the agreement would not be implemented, the Sykes-Picot agreement was indeed one of the fundamental events in the creation of the new Middle East, both because of how it was perceived in the Arab world and the realities it created. In the agreement, both England and France ignored ethnic and religious realities for the sake of their strategic interests; the possibility that one of these countries the deal would end up creating could be independent was beside the point. In fact, the dominant racial discourse at the time certainly made it ridiculous for Europeans to mention such independence. The belief that, all in all, the Arab nations were incapable of governing themselves was the accepted norm that explained why the British never really thought of their agreement with the Arabs too seriously. In the Arab world, the agreement was (and is still) seen as the culminating point of European, and by extension Western, perfidy. This central importance was most recently illustrated two years before the 100 anniversary of the deal as the so-called Islamic State referred to the agreement in a video dubbed "The End of Sykes-Picot." In its twisted way, the group indeed understood that these borders had never truly been accepted by the former subjects of the Ottoman Empire.

Sykes

Picot

The fall of the Ottoman Empire set the political and geostrategic scene of the new Middle East. In 1920, two years after the end of the war, the region was already experiencing growing instability. The issues and trends that would plague the region until today were growing. On April 4, Arab riots broke out in Jerusalem, fueled by the growing hostility against the Zionist movement. The British passivity would convince one of the Jewish leaders, Vladimir Jabotinsky (the future founder of the Israeli right-wing), of the strategic necessity of a strong Jewish military as the core of the future state.

Jabotinsky

Just two weeks later in Turkey, the Grand National Assembly in Ankara set the foundation of the Turkish state, opening the way for 8 years of reforms. In Iraq, a Shiite revolt broke out in the south, as locals demanded the creation of an Islamic state. The British compromise was to place Faisal, the son of Sharif Hussein and a Sunni, on the throne. His father, meanwhile, was embroiled in a conflict with a local tribe, the Ibn Saud, that sought to carve a new kingdom in the Arabian Peninsula.

More broadly, the long decline of the "sick man of Europe" fostered the emergence of nationalistic and ideological movements that are still key to any understanding of the Middle East today. The compatibility between the Islamic religion and culture and Western reforms were first discussed within the Empire, and they are still up for debate today. Abdul Hamid's pan-Islamism, while its results at the time remain limited, still resonates within the Muslim world and can still be seen as a viable rival to the region's various nationalistic aspirations.

In fact, almost 100 years after the fall of the Ottoman Empire, it is clear that the emergence of secular Arab nationalism triggered an opposite reaction from supporters of a political Islam and vice versa. The Muslim Brotherhood, for instance, was created as a reaction to the abolition of the Caliphate by Turkey in 1928 and would strengthen its ranks by being a viable opponent to the rising secular Arab nationalism. These mechanics are still at work today, as an initial wave of secular revolutions, the Arab Spring, triggered a second wave of "Green Revolutions." In parallel, whether in its most radical form with ISIS and al-Qaeda's idea of a Caliphate, or in the moderate ideology with the emergence of political Islam, Islam is still seen as an effective weapon against Western influence. In Turkey itself, the opposition between partisans of a strong Islamic identity and those such as Mustafa Kemal, who rejected it, still divides the political and social landscape.

These challenges, divides, and conflicts all stem from the power vacuum slowly left by the once powerful Ottoman Empire.

Online Resources

Other books about Middle East history by Charles River Editors

Other books about the Ottomans on Amazon

Bibliography

Abou-El-Haj, Rifa'at Ali (1984). The 1703 Rebellion and the Structure of Ottoman Politics. Istanbul: Nederlands Historisch-Archaeologisch Instituut te İstanbul.

Ahmad, Feroz. The Young Turks: The Committee of Union and Progress in Turkish Politics, 1908–1914, (1969).

Aziz Basan, Osman, Great Seljuks, Taylor & Francis, 2010.

Babinger, Franz, Mehmed the Conqueror and his time, Princeton University Press, 1992.

Bein, Amit. Ottoman Ulema, Turkish Republic: Agents of Change and Guardians of Tradition (2011) Amazon.com

Bonner, Michael, et al., Islam in the Middle Ages, Praeger Publishers, 2009.

Cleveland, William L, A History of the Modern Middle East, Westview Press, 2000.

Erickson, Edward J. Ordered to Die: A History of the Ottoman Army in the First World War (2000) Amazon.com, excerpt and text search

Goodwin, Jason, Lords of the Horizons, Vintage books, 1999.

Howard, Douglas A, A History of the Ottoman Empire, Cambridge University Press, 2017.

Kafadar, Cemal, Between Two Worlds: The Construction of the Ottoman State, University of California Press, 1995.

Karlsson, Ingmar, Turkiets historia, Historiska media, 2015.

Karpat, Kemal H. The Politicization of Islam: Reconstructing Identity, State, Faith, and Community in the Late Ottoman State. (2001). 533 pp.

Kunt, Metin İ. (1983). The Sultan's Servants: The Transformation of Ottoman Provincial Government, 1550-1650. New York: Columbia University Press. ISBN 0-231-05578-1.

Maalouf, Amin, Korstågen enligt araberna, Alhambra, 2004.

Mango, Cyril A, The Oxford History of Byzantium, Oxford University Press, 2002

McCarthy, Justin. The Ottoman Peoples and the End of Empire. Hodder Arnold, 2001. ISBN 0-340-70657-0.

McKay, John P., et al., A History of World Societies, Bedford/St Martins, 2014.

Nationalencyklopedien, NE, 2009.

Peirce, Leslie (1993). The Imperial Harem: Women and Sovereignty in the Ottoman Empire. Oxford: Oxford University Press. ISBN 0-19-508677-5.

Runciman, Steven, The Fall of Constantinople, Cambridge Press, 1969.

Tezcan, Baki (2010). The Second Ottoman Empire: Political and Social Transformation in the Early Modern World. Cambridge: Cambridge University Press. ISBN 978-1-107-41144-9.

Uyar, Mesut & Edward J. Erickson, A Military History of the Ottomans, Praeger Publishers, 2009.

Villads Jensen, Kurt, Korståg: européer i heligt krig under 500 år, Dialogos, 2017.

Free Books by Charles River Editors

We have brand new titles available for free most days of the week. To see which of our titles are currently free, click on this link.

Discounted Books by Charles River Editors

We have titles at a discount price of just 99 cents everyday. To see which of our titles are currently 99 cents, click on this link.

Made in the USA
San Bernardino, CA
01 December 2018